Forgiveness and Atonement

H. D. McDonald

Baker Book House

Grand Rapids, Michigan 49506

Other books by H. D. McDonald:

Ideas of Revelation, 1700–1860
Theories of Revelation, 1860–1960
I and He
Jesus—Human and Divine
Living Doctrines of the New Testament
Faith and Freedom: A Commentary on Paul's Epistle to the Galatians
The Church and Its Glory: Commentary on Ephesians
Commentary on Colossians and Philemon
What the Bible Teaches about Scripture
The Christian View of Man
Salvation
God and His World (forthcoming)

Copyright 1984 by
Baker Book House Company

ISBN: 0–8010–6165–2

Library of Congress Catalog Card Number 84–70507

Printed in the United States of America

Contents

1

Forgiveness: The Necessity and Possibility

The idea of the forgiveness of sins is central in the Christian message. Perhaps no other theme better sums up the content and reaches of the gospel than this. After his resurrection Jesus warmed the hearts of his disciples as he expounded to them the Scriptures which climaxed with the reassuring declaration that "repentance and forgiveness of sins should be preached in his name to all nations, beginning from Jerusalem" (Luke 24:47). The first preachers of the gospel proclaimed that Jesus, whom the people of Israel had killed by hanging on a tree, was exalted of God as Prince and Savior "to give repentance to Israel and forgiveness of sins" (Acts 5:31). And Paul was sent beyond the Jewish race to open the eyes of the Gentiles, turning them from darkness to light and from the power of Satan to God, that they might "receive forgiveness of sins and a place among those who are sanctified by faith" in Jesus (Acts 26:18).

Christianity, then, can aptly be designated the gospel of forgiveness, and it is rightly said that one of its chief creedal affirmations is, "I believe in the forgiveness of sins." The forgiveness of sins is indeed one of the main foci from which to contemplate the whole panorama of Christian truth. In the experience of forgiveness there unite all the grand themes of

7

divine revelation which systematic theology elaborates under its various headings. Around this truth every other foundational truth of the gospel may conveniently be grouped. For, as H. R. Mackintosh says, "No man can properly be ranked as a Christian, in the sense of the New Testament, who has not received the forgiveness of sins, or who is not conscious that through its impartation something has happened of decisive moment for his relation to God."[1] Or, as Luther more crisply declares, "Where forgiveness of sins is, there is life and blessedness."

Yet this message of the forgiveness of sins sounds hollow to modern ears. The moral man sees no need for forgiveness, and the philosophical man denies the possibility of it. Both positions hold that the very idea of the forgiveness of sins dwarfs man's stature and status in the universe as a moral and rational being. For instead of being able to fulfil the measure of his own duty or being the master of his own destiny man is presented in this gospel of forgiveness as a cringing animal and a helpless brute.

Two questions, then, must be discussed in our consideration of forgiveness: (1) Is the forgiveness of sin really necessary? and (2) Is forgiveness really possible?

Is Forgiveness of Sin Really Necessary?

Without doubt the enduring appeal that the gospel of Christ has had throughout past generations, and the joyous relief it has brought to burdened souls, are to be attributed to its assurance of divine forgiveness. In our day, however, it seems that this precious appeal fails to attract the attention of the average person or to stir the mass of the people with any deep interest. One of the chief reasons humans do not readily embrace the good news of God's forgiveness is that they do not believe they have done anything so wrong that they should seek it. For to ask for forgiveness would be to acknowledge the need of it, something most people are unable or unwilling to admit. They think with Walt Whitman that, as animals do not lie awake at night and weep for their sins, neither need they.

---

[1]H. R. Mackintosh, *The Christian Experience of Forgiveness* (London: Nisbet, 1927), p. 2.

Those to whom religious experience is foreign and who are yet interested in humanity and who labor to hasten mankind's progress consider the idea of forgiveness to be an antiquated way of understanding the nature of man and of stating his fundamental need. To such people the religious concept of sin is not something to be brooded over but rather something to be worked off, if not indeed shrugged off. After all, it is at worst nothing more than a morbid complex, the product of a faulty heredity, an unwholesome environment, or bad education. To the social reformer who views man in social units, the concept of the forgiveness of sins appears a rather pointless notion. Sin does not so much need to be forgiven as destroyed by eradicating its psychological or sociological causes. And this, the reformer thinks, can be brought about by the evolution of a new and higher type of humanity.

Yet despite all the protestations of modern men and women against the idea that they are sinful creatures needing forgiveness, there is a permanent and persistent suspicion that all is not well in the human condition. There is a feeling, pitiless and irresistible, that there is something at the very heart of things working against our best endeavors and highest aspirations, throwing us back aghast at our powerlessness to change and remedy the gaping inequities and injustices inherent in every political and industrial system. There is a radical twist in the very constitution of the universe which defeats our hopes, plays havoc with our dreams, and deflates our pathetic optimism. Many are aware that socially and nationally there is more of man's inhumanity to man today than at any other time in history and that somehow they are responsible for it. Thus, ironically, while the capacity for and the habit of penitence may have faded from the contemporary scene, there is a grave and keen sense in which they are present as never before.

While giving rise to feelings of inadequacy and frustration, awareness of the dire human condition can provide an impetus to social responsibility as well and can also become, like the law of old, a schoolmaster to bring men to Christ (Gal. 3:24–25). It can do so once we accept our measure of responsibility for the human condition and recognize that it is due in part to our own lack of goodness. To one who has reached this point the question must sooner or later pose itself, But why be good? What is the good of goodness anyway? For if there is no end, no plan, no absolute requirement, why bother? If goodness be not more fundamental, more worthwhile, more eternal than evil, whence come the sense of unease at the rampant display of evil, and the feeling of disquiet when truth and right and goodness are held back and flouted? One cannot then escape the conclusion that there must be a final truth, right, and good; there must indeed be a God. So must every wrong, and one's own most surely, be against this ultimate truth, right, and good, and thus be sin against God. To accept that there is such a moral being and still to affirm that one has no need of forgiveness will be unthinkable. For forgiveness becomes a spiritual and moral necessity once an individual recognizes personal responsibility for the breach in relationship with God due to failure to fulfil the purpose for which he or she was created. "The assurance of forgiveness becomes a spiritual necessity as soon as sin is conceived as a breach of fellowship with a divine person."[2]

If sin is conceived as an infirmity, or a mistake, or ignorance, or merely a stage in man's development, forgiveness would not be, as Christ's gospel declares it to be, an imperative of religious experience. Note, however, that it is to man as a sinful being that the revelation of God is uniformly addressed. Scripture eloquently declares the reality of sin as a personal and universal evil, while the divine grace offered to the human individual in the form of forgiveness is specifically adapted to his need as a sinful being. Some years ago a prolonged correspondence was conducted in *The Times* of London on the question, What is wrong with the world? The discussion was abruptly ended by a very brief letter:

> What's wrong with the world? Sir, I am!
>
> G. K. Chesterton

While it is not our purpose to detail the biblical teaching about sin, it is necessary that we give some account of it since we will be unable to get a right view of forgiveness until we

[2]E. Y. Mullins, *The Christian Religion in Its Doctrinal Expression* (Valley Forge, Pa.: Judson, 1917), p. 52.

first get a clear insight into the fact that there exists something real and tragic about man's condition which needs to be forgiven, something in which every individual is personally involved. What then is this thing called "sin" which the Christian gospel asserts must be forgiven and which Christian experience assures us can be? We must confine ourselves to this precise question, leaving aside cognate matters such as, How did sin enter the world? or How do we account for its spread over the whole area of human life? Such questions are, of course, important and call for discussion elsewhere. Our concern is, however, with that characteristic of sin that makes forgiveness a necessity if man is to regain a sense of fellowship with God (the purpose for which man was brought into existence) and so enjoy God forever.

The empirical reality of sin is omnipresent in the Old Testament Scriptures. It is depicted there as a universal phenomenon (see, e.g., 1 Kings 8:46; Ps. 143:2; Prov. 20:9; Eccles. 7:20, etc.). From the very first appearance of man on the stage of history as a sinner, sin's tragic effects on the I-Thou relationship between God and man and between man and man are clearly visible. The Old Testament uses several words to describe the awful reality of human wrongdoing. These words indicate that sin is a missing of the mark as regards God's purpose. In substance it is an attitude of resistance to God; in result it is a state of moral perversion which merits the judgment of God. All sin is an act against God. It is not just mere disregard of some legal requirement, nor the transgression of some ethical code. "Against thee, thee only, have I sinned" (Ps. 51:4). Sin is in essence a rupture in the personal relationship between God and man. It is a severance of the unseen ties between him and us. God turns away from the evil in which man has embroiled himself. The great prophets depict the sins of Israel as offenses against specific attributes of God. Isaiah, for example, stresses that sin is an offense against God's righteousness, and Hosea pictures it as a rejection of God's love. The deep sense of sin which pervades the Psalms does not arise merely from a fear of punishment, but from the recognition that sin brings a breach in our fellowship with God, for it causes him to hide his face and withdraw his mercies. Throughout the Old

Testament we find that while the form of sin varies, its essence as ultimately an act against God is unchanged. This one factor remains constant: "Sin is full of the sense of *wrong towards God.*"[3]

The words and presence of Jesus among men also emphasized the fact that in essence sin is wrong towards God. For Jesus, sin was willful wrongdoing, a lack of faith in and love for God. In this light it is clear that the exceeding gravity of sin lies in its being a direct offense against the character of God. This means that since Jesus Christ has been here, the hues of sin appear all the darker. Moreover, although he revealed sin's nature basically by denouncing its external manifestations, he strongly emphasized its inwardness. Sin has its seat in the human heart, in the inmost sanctuary of the personal life. The individual heart is the hidden laboratory where the poison of sin is brewed by each man. According to Jesus, man is defiled, not by what comes from without, but by what comes from within (Matt. 15:11; Mark 7:15; see Matt. 9:4; Mark 3:5). The outside of the cup of life may be washed clean, while the life within is full of extortion and rapacity (Matt. 23:27). A show of righteousness may go hand in hand with a heart full of hypocrisy and iniquity (Matt. 23:28). By such remarks Jesus traces sin right down to the inner being of man, to the springs of his motives and desires. The tree of life is poisoned at the roots, and its growth is finally and fatally stunted by sin's hurtful influence.

It is not, of course, easy for a man to admit that he is a sinner or that deep down in his inmost being reigns something which renders his real selfhood crooked and perverse. Occasional glimpses of his true state he may have, but these tend to be so fleeting and passing as not to have lasting effect. People may indeed, as Søren Kierkegaard declares, get a *feeling* of helplessness during a Sunday sermon, but for the rest of the week they regard themselves able to manage on their own.[4] No pressure social or circumstantial will convince

[3]Stewart A. McDowall, *Is Sin Our Fault?* (London: Hodder & Stoughton, 1932), p. 210.

[4]Søren Kierkegaard, *Concluding Unscientific Postscript*, trans. David Swenson and Walter Lowrie (Princeton, N.J.: Princeton University, 1944), p. 419.

a man of his own inner deficiency. For even if his whole world were to come crashing down upon him, he would still harbor the belief that he was but the victim of ill fortune and that he could rise again. It is only in the recognition of failure in the innermost depths of one's own person that there is sufficient persuasive revelation of one's true condition to put him on course toward seeking God's forgiveness.

Thus it is only under the white light of Jesus' own sinless life that the true nature of our sin is by contrast disclosed. There was no rupture in his personal relationship with God his Father. He was himself, in the days of his flesh, assailed by the temptations of the world, the flesh, and the devil; but he triumphantly endured them, and throughout them all maintained the integrity of his soul. Therefore, "if any deep meaning of the character and life of Jesus is understood, if the attraction of this life appears as the very life and meaning of our own souls, then there can only result deep perplexity, sorrow, and pain at the disclosure of the falling short, and the actual contradiction of our own nature."[5] In the presence of Jesus, seen for who he is as the holy one of God, man finds himself a sinner, and comes to recognize sin for what it is, as a provocation of the righteous, just, and holy God. There under the searching light of Christ's pure life a man must acknowledge responsibility for his own soiled nature and realize the horror of sin.

It is, then, "in the light of Christ that we see sin clearly and can in some real degree understand how it looks to God, whose estimate of it we are bound to share so far as we discover it. In proportion as a man grows familiar with the fact of Christ and lets the illumination of that pure spirit fall on his own soiled nature, he will become more sensitive to the horror of sin; also with growing insight he will discriminate more surely what is sin from what is not."[6] It is because God's holiness and love have come near to us in Christ that we can see sin for the evil thing it is. For in his near-

<hr>

[5]W. E. Orchard, *Modern Theories of Sin* (London: James Clarke, 1909), p. 143.

[6]Mackintosh, *Christian Experience*, pp. 53–54.

ness to us we become aware of his distance from us and thus learn that "sin is the perversion of human nature through the perversion of the human attitude towards God."[7]

But it is only in the cross of the suffering Christ that we can finally estimate the measure and depth of sin as God sees it. Only here, by the means he willed, can the conscience of man learn something of sin's awfulness as an objective reality. The cross was not just an act of an unruly Jewish mob and a few muddle-headed religious and national leaders. It was humanity's act; it was our act. We were there when they crucified the Lord of glory. What they did we all have done—crucified Christ afresh. For it was sin that nailed him to the tree; sin that did the deed, the sin of every single one of us. The night on which Jesus was betrayed, the hour at which he was crucified, the whole human race learned what sin is and that we are all sinners. Not only Judas, but all of us, betrayed the Lord; not only Roman soldiers, but each one of us, pierced his side.

So it is shown, as P. T. Forsyth says, that "the moral difficulty of society is not that we are strayed children, great babes in the wood. It is that we are sinful men in a sinful world."[8] If, then, modern man is not worrying about his sins, it is because modern man has never seriously contemplated Golgotha. For no man can stand in the shadow of that cross and still delude himself into imagining that sin does not matter. Calvary makes clear once and forever that it matters decisively for each one of us and it matters terribly to God. If yet a man proclaims his own self-sufficiency and insists that he has no need of forgiveness, all that can be said to him is the retort of Anselm of Canterbury: *Nondum considerasti quanti ponderis sit peccatum* ("Not yet hast thou considered the gravity of sin"). For the truth of the matter is, as runs the refrain with which Kierkegaard ends each of his seven Joyful Notes in the Strife of Suffering, "Sin alone is man's ruin." John Owen's remark can then be given full credence: "He

---

[7]Emil Brunner, *The Mediator* (London: Lutterworth, 1934), p. 443.

[8]P. T. Forsyth, *Positive Preaching and the Modern Mind* (London: Hodder & Stoughton, 1909), p. 342.

who has slight thoughts of sin, had never great thoughts of God."[9]

Is Forgiveness of Sin Really Possible?

The second question which requires consideration is, Is forgiveness of sin really possible? Many emphatically maintain that it is not, because the whole of man's existence—the moral no less than the physical, the spiritual no less than the natural—is under the dominion of inevitable law. An inflexible moral sanction pervades the total order so that the deed once done can never be undone. In the words of T. H. Huxley, there can be no back moves. Nothing, absolutely nothing, can right one's past wrong. In the declaration, "What I have written, I have written," Pilate gave voice to this concept of unchangeableness and finality. The writing remains forever, for the legend cannot be rewritten; its letters cannot be erased. Such is the essence of Omar Khayyam's oft-quoted lines:

> The Moving Finger writes; and, having writ,
> Moves on: nor all your Piety nor Wit
> Shall lure it back to cancel half a line,
> Nor all your Tears wash out a Word of it.

Modern dramatists and novelists have produced many works reflecting their conviction of the truth of this idea. And the foremost realistic writers of our times have sought to unveil the implications which the concept of unchangeableness has for the soul. Some of them describe a process of moral deterioration. A man who sets out deliberately to flout his innate sense of right comes at length to lose all moral vision and sensitivity. He refuses to follow the light, and for him the light ceases to shine. So he walks in darkness. Relentlessly and inexorably the end of that man is moral suicide. Nothing and no one, it is proclaimed, can restore to such a man his moral susceptibility. His capacity for goodness has been

[9]John Owen, *The Forgiveness of Sin* (reprint, Grand Rapids: Baker, 1977), p. 84.

forever lost. To speak of forgiveness for such a man is pointless if it means there is pardon for him; it would be even more pointless if our concept of forgiveness entails a promise of restoration. Before the moral law under which he has lived, even the love and mercy of God are powerless to interpose.

Other writers have created characters whose moral lapses are but isolated occasions to be regretted rather than the first step in a process of total deterioration. In an unguarded moment a man set on a course of moral rectitude is swept off his feet by a surging passion which he may at once acknowledge as his failure to live up to his own standards. Indeed, in the aftermath of the experience, when the conscience is again alert and the ideal appears beckoningly before him once more, he may even admit the failure with sorrow and shame. But in no way will he regard his lapse as something for which he should seek the forgiveness of God. He will resent the suggestion that by some act of God the deed can be pardoned and the slate wiped clean. He will protest that the act was his own, and that not even God can treat it as something which has not happened and from which he can hide his face. For that would be, he surmises, to make God less moral than himself. He did the deed and he must bear the consequences. The man of moral sensitivity and standards will not be persuaded that he will not have to pay for his past somehow, if only in the here and now.

The objections to divine forgiveness on the grounds that the moral order reacts to sin with the same inexorability as does the natural law, and that the effects of sin are irreversible, will not easily be dispelled by reasoned argument. Indeed, there are two facts implied in the contention which must be acknowledged as authentic enough. The one is that there is no forgiveness in nature. Punishment, not forgiveness, appears to be inevitable in the divine order when we violate its laws. Emil Brunner is therefore right in declaring that "forgiveness is the very opposite of anything which can be taken for granted. Nothing is less obvious than forgiveness."[10] A page later he reaffirms, "But if any truth is obvious certainly it is not forgiveness but punishment."[11]

[10]Brunner, *Mediator*, p. 448.
[11]Ibid., p. 449.

The other implication which must be acknowledged is that the forgiveness of God does not mean the canceling of consequences. While it is a certainty of Christian experience that the eternal consequences of sin—forfeiture of fellowship with God—divine forgiveness does remit and remove, there are other areas, physical and environmental, from which the consequences of wrongdoing are not magically swept away. Something of their awful ramifications do remain and perhaps will remain forever. Alexander Whyte, commenting on the evildoing of some Old Testament characters, observes, "While they were forgiven for it, the vengeance which was taken on it, and on them, broke every bone of their body and every hard spot in their hearts."[12] It must be allowed, then, that as a happening and action in the past the evil deed is unalterable. God "cannot undo the sin, but he can forgive the sinner."[13] Still, this does not make forgiveness any the less credible or less wonderful, but rather more so. For "in a spiritually constituted world we are not shut up to believe that sin must entail final or hopeless fatalities of evil consequences."[14] The one whose past is forgiven may derive from it lessons and values of highest worth which will affect for good his future conduct. For even out of man's darkest deed and foulest sin God can bring good.

But the basic objection that God's forgiveness is not possible because of the unseverable cause-effect connection between evil and punishment remains. The whole structure of life is such that wrongdoing will be found out, and no exemption from its effects can intervene. This contention, however, is not valid. For even the ordering of the natural realm by law does not prohibit God's further and special acting. If this were an apologetic for miracles we would endeavor to show that the Humean view of reality is not ultimate. True, nature does behave in a regular fashion according to certain laws. But then, as Karl Barth declares,

[12]Alexander Whyte, *Bible Characters: Gideon to Absalom* (London: Oliphants, n.d.), p. 61.

[13]W. N. Clarke, *An Outline of Christian Theology* (Edinburgh: T. & T. Clark, 1903), p. 256.

[14]Mackintosh, *Christian Experience*, p. 11.

"we cannot hypostatise the concept of law."[15] Laws are not the final factor in the universe. Behind the interlocking system of nature is a personal God who can act directly in his own universe and can inaugurate irregular happenings in the broad scheme of regular events. The evidences for the uniformity of nature are there, but there are also evidences that God intervenes in his world. Thus the basic uniformity does not exclude God but, on the contrary, points to him, for were there no settled order, there would be no miracles. Miracles, in fact, presuppose law; and they offer proof of the existence of nature's uniformity. But uniformity is not mechanism, for nature is a vast realm of life and meaning whose final unity is to be found in the living and personal God. We must, therefore, as William James urges, rid ourselves of the mechanical and impersonal view of the ultimate.

The realities of everyday life, such as the free activities of thought, choice, and love, show plainly that there is much that is not under the dominion of inevitable law. These realities take place in a uniform world without violating the natural order. Man can act freely in an ordered universe. He can by the operation of his own volition bring about results which would not have come about without his willing. It cannot, therefore, be impossible for God, who is the source and cause of that voluntary ability in man, to act immediately in and work directly on that system of nature which he himself has created and now sustains.

That there is an inevitable conjunction between sin and judgment is granted. But this does not render it impossible for God to act in forgiveness. For God can bend the law by a veritable miracle to bring about sin's remission and to deal with it in the grace of forgiveness. For forgiveness is truly a miracle of God in the ordered realm of moral existence. It is the man or woman who has had a personal consciousness of sin and a living experience of its forgiveness who is best qualified to treat the subject of miracles. Such a one already has an assurance in his or her own life of an "intervention" of God into human affairs which does not abrogate the law of cause and effect. God's greatest act is his providing of forgiveness, the grace of his pardon, for humans in a manner

[15]Karl Barth, *Church Dogmatics* (Edinburgh: T. & T. Clark, 1975), 3.3:129.

consistent with the laws of nature and therefore with the ultimate moral principles of its operation. In the end it is by a miracle that we are redeemed into an understanding of the miraculous. Only one who has experienced a miracle can truly believe in a miracle.

Brunner stresses the miraculous quality of forgiveness:

> But this means that forgiveness can only take place as a real divine act. The sense of acceptance, the certainty of forgiveness, can only legitimately refer to a divine act of revelation, to an explicit communication of this divine secret. Such an act would be the most inconceivable revelation possible, something so new that it could never be imagined. Further, this forgiveness would have to be imparted in such a way that the holiness of God, the inviolability of the law and the logical demands of the penal order would still be maintained. Thus the perfect revelation of forgiveness can only be such as brings out with intense emphasis that it cannot and must not be taken for granted. This means that it must be of such a kind that it will express the reality of guilt, the reality of the divine wrath, and yet, at the same time, the overwhelming reality of forgiving love.[16]

That justice can be satisfied and sins remitted is, indeed, as Kierkegaard declares, the "paradox of forgiveness."[17] P. T. Forsyth asks the question, "Is not God's forgiveness the great moral paradox, the great incredibility of the moral life, needing all the miracle of Christ's person and action to make us realize it when we grasp the terms?"[18] Yes, it most certainly is. God's "holy forgiveness is the greatest moral paradox, the most exalting, pacifying paradox, the greatest practical paradox, in the world."[19]

It will not do, then, to proclaim that God cannot forgive, and forgive in a manner which befits him and is consistent with his total nature. Man's relation to God is not finally or fully expressed in legalistic, but in personal, terms. God does,

---

[16]Brunner, *Mediator*, p. 449.

[17]Kierkegaard, *Postscript*, p. 210.

[18]Forsyth, *Positive Preaching*, p. 290; cf. Kierkegaard, *Postscript*, pp. 210–14.

[19]Forsyth, *Positive Preaching*, pp. 299–300.

of course, stand in relation to man in nature, but as man's
Creator and Judge; in grace, however, his relation to man is
that of Redeemer and Father. In that relationship he forgives.
On the human level, in the personal relation of man to man,
and especially in the more intimate relation of parent to
child, forgiveness is a necessary principle of social well-being.
That one should in certain circumstances forgive another
seems to be an innate element of the human spirit. "We
ourselves are prompted by our nature, as well as by the
precepts of revelation, to forgive an offender; and there is a
demand in the very constitution of our souls which is not met
if this is never done."[20] It is a veritable law of our being that
forgiveness should be extended to the wrongdoer. There is
something native to the human individual which calls for the
exercise of sympathy as well as justice. There are occasions
when the offended person is compelled by considerations
within himself to show compassion to the one by whom he
has been hurt. And when we see such demonstrations of
sympathy and compassion in the forgiveness of another for a
wrong done, we recognize it as a quality godlike and divine.
Since "God has implanted this feeling so deeply in the human
soul, and made the manifestation of it so essential to the good
of society, may it be not inferred that it is a principle of his
own nature and in his own administrations? Would he make
necessary in a human government a principle which has no
place in his own? Would he implant in the human soul what
has no counterpart in his own nature?"[21] A disposition to
forgive, the quality of sympathy—these must surely be found
in God; in his administration there must be an arrangement
for their exercise.

We must not, however, too glibly admit into consideration
this human instinct to forgive in considering the forgiveness
of God. It is not the case that there is something automatic
about God's forgiveness or that there is some conditioning
"must" which compels him to do no other. "Mercy and
pardon do not come forth from God," says John Owen, "as

[20]Albert Barnes, *The Atonement* (reprint, Minneapolis: Bethany Fellowship, n.d.), p. 33.
[21]Ibid., p. 37.

light from the sun, or water from the sea, by a necessary consequence of their natures, whether they will or not. It does not necessarily follow that any one must be made partaker of forgiveness because God is infinitely gracious: for may he not do what he will with his own?"[22] We must not then think of God as under some sort of moral necessity to forgive. It is in fact the moral man who is least disposed to forgive. "The natural man either does not forgive—and there are none more unforgiving than sticklers for morality; or else he forgives as he shaves—'I suppose I ought to'; or as he dines—'because I like to.'"[23] It must then be remembered that

> this experience, as between man and man, is not in itself a revelation or discovery of God. It does not take us all the way. For one thing, man's pardon of man is sharply limited to the circumstances of a particular offence; it does not and cannot cover the man's whole life. No one can forgive his neighbour's sin. What appears to me in others as pure goodness does make clearer to me the fact that goodness alone can help me; yet it is just this goodness which erects a barrier between me and these benefactors, and renders them incapable of meeting my sorest need. Our sin, indeed, may come to blind us utterly to the human goodness we once perceived, and quench in us the trust and reverence it had evoked. For another thing, man's power to forgive man is undermined by his own sinfulness, which leaves him with nothing more than ability to condone this or that particular fault or shortcoming. The goodness we are conscious of in others is invariably submerged again in our awareness of their sin, and we are left in doubt whether what we have before us is moral personality in the strict sense or only a certain blossoming of natural good temper.[24]

God is neither a sort of genial superman nor a remote unconcerned deity. He does not and cannot forgive sin with an unholy ease. Yet he does and can forgive in righteous love. The truth is thus "midway between the Pelagian view, that there is no obstacle to the forgiveness of sins, and the modern

[22]Owen, *Forgiveness*, p. 92.
[23]Forsyth, *Positive Preaching*, p. 300.
[24]Mackintosh, *Christian Experience*, pp. 46, 47.

rationalistic view, that since law fully expresses God there is no forgiveness of sins at all."[25]

Only in revelation, and in the experience of that revelation, is God known as the forgiver of sins. God is Creator and Judge, and in that relation he may and must exercise justice; he is also Father and Redeemer, and in that relation he can and does exercise forgiveness. Yet these two aspects of God are not at odds. God is not at war with himself, for he is one. He is at once Creator and Father, Judge and Redeemer.

Herein is the dialectical tension of the gospel: man's sinfulness—God as Judge; man's forgiveness—God as Redeemer. "That," says Kierkegaard, "is really profound in Christianity: Christ is both our Saviour and our Judge, not that there is one saviour and one judge, for then we would certainly be sentenced, but that the Saviour and the Judge are one."[26]

[25]A. H. Strong, *Systematic Theology* (New York: A. C. Armstrong, 1889), p. 282.

[26]Quoted in Louis Dupré, *Kierkegaard as Theologian* (London: Sheed and Ward, 1964), p. 91.

2

Revelation and Forgiveness

Nature and Forgiveness

Towards the end of the previous chapter it was suggested that the idea of forgiveness is not derived from nature. It is not a conclusion drawn from natural theology, nor a discovery of the human mind as it contemplates the natural rhythm of things. The "order of things is dead against the thought of forgiveness, for there is not a hint of it in Nature, or at all events the half-decipherable hints which Nature may contain are illegible by any mind not already enlightened by the experience of being personally pardoned."[1] It may indeed be allowed that an inductive reading of nature's history and purpose does give some evidence of a higher benignity and a providential care. And there may be moments "beautiful and rare" when a man can catch, within and behind the grandeur and glory of the natural universe, a grander glory; there may be moments when he has a glimpse of the Beyond that is within.

But this vision will not convey a sense of forgiveness to him or encourage him to believe that his failure to conduct himself in the world according to the dictates of his moral self

[1]H. R. Mackintosh, *The Christian Experience of Forgiveness* (London: Nisbet, 1927), pp. 89–90.

can go unpunished. Nature as it confronts man as a sinner is really heartlessly ambiguous in this regard. For if some signs of mercy are detectable in the phenomenon of nature, there are others which can only show it either as utterly indifferent or crassly cruel. Thomas Browne's view of nature in his *Religio Medici* as "the art of God" can be counterbalanced by that of Tennyson in his *In Memoriam*—"Nature, red in tooth and claw." And "we are told that Nature never restores order where disorder has occurred. 'Shuffling,' said Professor Eddington, is the thing Nature never undoes."[2]

The laws of nature are, in truth, like Mark Rutherford's Mrs. Snale, "cruel, not with the ferocity of the tiger but with the dull insensibility of a cart wheel, which runs over a man's neck as easily as over a flint." It is truly "not easy to perceive there any law or order which proceeds from God of whose character Christian faith tells us in Christ. This is a rational world, but it is not plainly a moral world, still less a world illustrating the high ethical and spiritual laws of the gospel."[3] Indeed, as C. S. Lewis remarks, "Nature has the air of a good thing spoiled."[4]

The order nature displays and the wonder it evokes at most reveal God's eternal power and deity (Rom. 1:20). Therefore, says John Owen, "the consideration of *his works* [i.e., nature] will not help a man to the knowledge that there is forgiveness with God."[5]

Liberal theology has laid great stress on the fact that God is Creator and that this is God's world. This is especially the case today, for it theologically justifies the contemporary preoccupation with ecology and universal social concern. By this insistence liberalism has, however, been led to conclude that God's fatherhood extends in the same way to all his relationships with all men. "Our religion," declares P. T. Forsyth, "understands better some aspects of the Father," but, he asks, "does it understand the only guarantee of His

[2]C. S. Lewis, *Miracles* (London: Bles, 1947), p. 181.

[3]P. Carnegie Simpson, *The Facts of Life* (London: Hodder & Stoughton, 1913), p. 30.

[4]Lewis, *Miracles*, p. 147.

[5]John Owen, *The Forgiveness of Sin* (reprint, Grand Rapids: Baker, 1977), p. 124.

fatherhood—the Redeemer?"[6] To place fatherhood in the forefront is to invert the true order of the relationship between natural and revealed theology. For the former, far from being a steppingstone to the latter, gets its credibility and illumination only from God's special unveiling. "Creation by itself is not grace, but is only seen to be grace retrospectively in the light of the Gospel and its grace, from the standpoint, that is to say, of a creature who has been called into living fellowship with God his Creator."[7] Sin destroys "the perceptibility of God in His works," so that "the revelation in creation is not sufficient in order to know God in such a way that this knowledge brings salvation."[8]

This is the truth to which John Masefield gives witness in his *Everlasting Mercy*. In this story Saul Kane had for some years "lived in disbelief of heaven." Then came the day when he found his inner thirst assuaged by "the drink unprised," from "the burning cataract of Christ." Masefield puts in unforgettable words the throbbing sense of the divine forgiveness which opened Kane's eyes to the glory of a world to which he had been hitherto blind.

> I did not think, I did not strive,
> The deep peace burnt my me alive;
> The bolted door had broken in,
> I knew that I had done with sin.
> I knew that Christ had given me birth
> To brother all the souls on earth,
> And every bird and every beast
> Should share the crumbs broke at the feast.
>
> O Glory of the lightened mind.
> How dead I'd been, how dumb, how blind.
> The station brook, to my new eyes,
> Was babbling out of Paradise;
> The waters rushing from the rain
> Were singing Christ has risen again.

[6]P. T. Forsyth, *The Person and Place of Jesus Christ* (London: Independent Press, 1946), p. 24.

[7]N. H. G. Robinson, *Christ and Conscience* (London: Nisbet, 1956), p. 102.

[8]Emil Brunner, "Nature and Grace," in *Natural Theology* (London: Bles, 1946), pp. 25–26.

I thought all earthly creatures knelt
From rapture of the joy I felt.
The narrow station-wall's brick ledge,
The wild hop withering in the hedge,
The light in huntsman's upper storey.
Were parts of an eternal glory,
Where God's eternal garden flowers.
I stood in bliss at this for hours.

Conscience and Forgiveness

Conscience is no more a witness to the possibility of forgiveness than is nature. According to John Owen, "conscience naturally knows nothing of forgiveness, it is against its very word and office, to hear anything of it."[9] What, then, is conscience? and What is its function?

For a true account of conscience we must, of course, turn to the New Testament and especially to Paul. It is Paul the Apostle rather than Freud the psychiatrist who has the right words to say on the subject. In Freud's view conscience is a thing acquired, a social creation which judges whether an act is acceptable within the community. This means that in Freud's exposition morality itself is a changeable and relative affair. But for Paul the Christian apostle, man *qua* man is a moral being with moral obligations and responsibilities. On this premise he argues with Felix "about justice and self-control and future judgment" (Acts 24:25). It is in relation to this understanding of the human individual that Paul develops the Christian view of conscience. In the possession of conscience by every man the apostle sees evidence of the universality and validity of man's moral nature. By his conscience man knows himself to be confronted with God's demands and judgments. Even pagan Gentiles who had no written law were aware of an inbuilt code written on their hearts. So each man is responsible for his own conduct.

Although the word *conscience* is used by the apostle twenty-one times, including twice in Acts (23:1; 24:16), it is absent from the Old Testament except in one instance in the

[9]Owen, *Forgiveness*, p. 27.

Septuagint (Eccles. 10:20), where the English translations have "thought." The exercise of conscience is, however, present throughout the Old Testament: in, for example, such statements as "David's heart smote him" (1 Sam. 24:15; 2 Sam. 24:10). Again, while the word does not appear in the teaching of Jesus, much of his teaching may be said to be concerned with the awakening of conscience by directing attention to the motive behind the overt act. The literal meaning of the Greek word for "conscience" *(syneidēsis)* is "joint-knowledge"; it appears to denote the reflective judgment which a man has alongside the original consciousness of an act. Paul certainly associates conscience with man's moral awareness (see, e.g., Acts 23:1; 24:16; Rom. 2:15; 9:1; 15:5). Possessing this natural faculty, man can judge whether or not his own actions accord with his innate moral sense (2 Cor. 1:12). Conscience "presents man as his own judge."[10]

Conscience is, therefore, a distinctive of human individuality as an inner witness to man's moral responsibility and the inherent capacity to distinguish between right and wrong. "There is," says Bishop Butler (Sermon 1), "a principle of reflection in [men] by which they distinguish between approval and disapproval of their own actions. . . . This principle . . . is conscience." Conscience is therefore to be understood as a native property of the human person. It is not to be conceived as a *donum superadditum*, a gift added to man's natural faculties. Nor is conscience to be spoken of as the intuitive "voice of God" within. It is certainly not the voice of God in the sense of an inner and immediate whispering from above. When the conscience stimulates a man to awareness of his sin and guilt, it may be referred to as the voice of God in a secondary sense. In this sense it is true that "the voice of God is above all the voice of conscience, but not in the sense that it is nothing but one's conscience; it is a divine refinement of the working of conscience."[11]

Dietrich Bonhoeffer stresses the self-judging role of con-

[10]B. F. Westcott, *Commentary on Hebrews* (London: Macmillan, 1892), p. 292.

[11]H. D. Lewis, *The Philosophy of Religion* (London: English Universities, 1965), p. 273.

science. Its chief concern he considers to be man's relation
with himself. "Conscience pretends to be the voice of God and
the standard for the relation to other men. It is therefore from
his right relation to himself that man is to recover the right
relation to God and to other men," and come to the awareness of good and evil. In goodness man had unity of self, but
in evil there came disunity. "Man has become the origin of
good and evil. He does not deny his evil; but in conscience
man summons himself, who has become evil, back to his
proper self, to good."[12] While we may in the process be stirred
by George Washington's purple description urging us to
"labour to keep alive in [our] breast that little spark of
celestial fire, called conscience,"[13] we are all more personally
aware of the truth of Hamlet's words, "Conscience doth make
cowards of us all."

In the conflict between right and wrong conscience acts as
umpire. But often so strong are the forces of evil that
conscience's judgments are unheeded; and not infrequently
the enemy is hardly identifiable. Evil comes upon a man "in
countless respectable and seductive disguises so that his
conscience becomes timid and unsure of itself, till in the end
he is satisfied if instead of a clear conscience he has a salved
one, and lies to his own conscience to avoid despair."[14] At the
same time, the man who would retain his own moral integrity as a person must respect conscience; he must, indeed,
follow its guidance.

In relation to forgiveness the conscience appears to act in a
twofold manner. On the one hand, in the natural man where
conscience is faithfully regarded there is usually occasion for
self-congratulation and little awareness of the need for forgiveness. "The call of conscience in natural man is the
attempt on the part of the ego to justify itself in its knowledge
of good and evil before God, before men, and before itself, and
to secure its own continuance in this self-justification."[15] A
man whose only authority is his conscience may feel satisfied
to have followed its dictates. He may in fact preen himself on

[12]D. Bonhoeffer, *Ethics* (London: SCM, 1955), p. 149.
[13]Jared Spark, *Life of Washington* (1839), vol. 2, p. 109.
[14]Bonhoeffer, *Ethics*, p. 5.
[15]Ibid., pp. 211–12.

his moral integrity and on his having achieved moral self-hood. "Thus the call of conscience has its origin and its goal in the autonomy of a man's own ego."[16] Accordingly, the natural man who manages to follow his conscience has a tendency to develop the most ungodly self-satisfaction along with self-sufficient rectitude. "Let self-righteousness be enthroned, and natural conscience desires no more; it is satisfied and pacified."[17] Thus, as Thomas Erskine of Linlathen says, "most men are so possessed of themselves that they have no vacuum in which God's deep water may arise."

On the other hand, when the conscience is not regarded and its voice is ignored, one reaches a position of moral insensitivity. By being ignored and transgressed it becomes "defiled" (1 Cor. 8:7), and so weakened (1 Cor. 8:12), or even "seared," and thus it is rendered insensible to goodness (1 Tim. 4:2). "To do wrong gives us a bad conscience, and a bad conscience paralyses moral nature."[18] By persistent wrongdoing the moral sense is dulled and induces the condition that Paul calls *nous adokimos* ("a reprobate mind," Rom. 1:28). There is no possibility of repentance (and, consequently, of forgiveness), for "the more we need to sorrow for our sins with a sorrow which reaches the depths of our nature with healing pain, the less sorrow is in our power."[19]

It is nevertheless folly to make light of conscience, for its power to punish sin is an accepted dictum among moralists.

> Conscience comes from the depth which lies beyond a man's own will and his own reason and it makes itself heard as the call of human existence to unity with itself. Conscience comes as an indictment of the loss of this unity and as a warning against the loss of one's self. Primarily it is directed not towards a particular kind of doing but towards a particular mode of being. It protests against a doing which imperils the unity of this being with itself.
>
> So long as conscience can be formally defined in these terms it is extremely inadvisable to act against its authority; disre-

[16]Ibid., p. 212.
[17]Owen, *Forgiveness*, p. 78.
[18]James Denney, *The Christian Doctrine of Reconciliation* (London: Hodder & Stoughton, 1918), p. 189.
[19]Ibid.

gard for the call of conscience will necessarily entail the destruction of one's own being, not even a purposeful surrender of it; it will bring about the decline and collapse of a human existence. Action against one's own conscience runs parallel with suicidal action against one's own life, and it is not by chance that the two often go together. Responsible action which did violence to conscience in this formal sense would indeed be reprehensible.[20]

That, however, is not by any means the whole story. For the power of conscience is limited. It is not enough to say, as some moralists and theologians do, that the guilt which follows an evil deed like a hangover is itself the punishment. It is one thing to say—and it is rightly said—that the consequences of wrongdoing are realized through conscience; but it is another thing to say—and that is wrongly said—that the two are identical. For the consequences of evil actions go far beyond the subjective awareness of guilt. There is the further reality of objective judgment, whether acknowledged or not. It is through one's conscience indeed that one "belongs to the moral world and can conceive such an idea as that of punishment; but though it is true to say that all punishment is through conscience, it is unreal to say that it is limited to conscience. The divine reaction against sin is instinctively understood by conscience, but in itself it is independent of it, and it may be most powerful and inexorable when the conscience is seared and unconscious of it."[21]

It is the conscience made sensitive by the action of the Holy Spirit which recognizes the true nature of the self behind all its expressions. But nonetheless conscience does not have a place of absolute authority, and is not finally the medium and standard of divine truth. Rashdall declares that "it is enough to insist that no one makes his submission to the teaching of our Lord Himself absolute and unconditional except in so far as the actual injunctions of that authority commend themselves to his conscience."[22] Although this is in a sense correct,

[20]Bonhoeffer, *Ethics*, p. 211.

[21]Denney, *Christian Doctrine*, p. 215.

[22]Hastings Rashdall, *Conscience and Christ*, 3d ed. (London: Duckworth, 1924), p. 33.

conscience is still not the medium of the apprehension of divine truth. That would accord it too high a status and take insufficient account of the searing effects of sin on it. Nor will it do to talk of the education of the conscience as though that would ensure apprehension of divine truth concerning ourselves. For the fact is that "the self in the position of viewing its own actions is not invariably expressing its own conscience."[23] This is but another way of saying that "our supreme need, therefore, is not the education of our conscience, not the absorption of our sin, nor even our reconciliation alone, but our redemption. It is not cheer that we need but salvation, not help but rescue, not a stimulus but a change, not tonics but life. Our one need of God is a moral need in the strictest, holiest sense. The best of nature can never meet it. It involves a new nature, a new world, a new creation. It is the moral need, not to be transformed, but to be saved."[24] This requirement has its beginning and end in the assurance of a divine forgiveness; therefore, for the relationship "between man and God the real bridge-head in the human world of the divine is not our conscience but Christ."[25]

Conscience indeed stands against the idea of forgiveness. As Otto Borchert says, "Forgiveness of sin contradicts the teaching of conscience."[26] It wishes to be the autocratic ruler of man's moral life, where it "labours to keep the whole domain, and keep the power of forgiveness from being enthroned in the soul."[27] The voice of conscience would drown all whisperings of hope. There is, however, another word that would be heeded: the divine declaration "To the Lord our God belong mercies and forgiveness, though we have rebelled against him" (Dan. 9:9, KJV).

Sound Christian theology is often better expressed in the church's hymnology than in the massive tomes of its speculative theologians. A perusal of the hymns of Charles Wesley,

[23]Reinhold Niebuhr, *The Self and the Dramas of History* (London: Faber & Faber, n.d.), p. 25.

[24]P. T. Forsyth, *Positive Preaching and the Modern Mind* (London: Hodder & Stoughton, 1909), p. 56.

[25]Robinson, *Christ and Conscience*, p. 62.

[26]Otto Borchert, *The Original Jesus*, trans. L. M. Stalker (London: Lutterworth, 1933), p. 368.

[27]Owen, *Forgiveness*, p, 78.

Isaac Watts, and Frances Ridley Havergal will sustain this
assertion. Another case in point is a bit of evangelistic jingle
which nevertheless carries an authentic message of divine
encouragement to the individual suffering from the tyranny
of conscience:

> Let not conscience make you linger,
>   Nor of fitness fondly dream;
> All the fitness He requireth
>   Is to feel your need of Him.

If, then, there is no witness in nature or in conscience to the
forgiveness of God, how does it happen that the Christian
preacher proclaims its possibility and Christian believers
rejoice in its experience?

Revelation and Forgiveness

Forgiveness is altogether a supernatural reality which has
its fount in the depths of God's eternal being. And everything
"that God does has an abyss of mystery in it, because it has
God in it."[28] Not, then, by the wisdom of man did it become
known that God forgives. It is a truth about God that comes
anōthen ("from above"). All those divine aspects of God
which include and are included in his forgiveness "can be
known *only by special revelation.*"[29] It is, therefore, to God's
self-affirming disclosure made perpetual and contemporary
in the biblical word that we have to turn for certainty and
assurance of God's forgiveness. As the Scriptures of truth, the
biblical word speaks of God and is where God speaks. In and
through this divine literature the living God is revealed. "He
is known through revelation alone. This Lord God is the God
of the biblical revelation."[30]

The word of divine forgiveness is the distinctive of the
biblical revelation. Other religions may have their high ethical concepts, but they know little of a God who forgives. In
Hinduism and Buddhism with their inexorable law of karma

[28]Austin Farrer, *Saving Faith* (London: Hodder & Stoughton, 1964), p. 99.
[29]Owen, *Forgiveness*, p. 123.
[30]Emil Brunner, *Revelation and Reason* (London: SCM, 1946), p. 44.

the possibility and wonder of forgiveness are absent, while the harsh justice of the Islamic Allah has no significant place for real forgiveness. But in biblical faith there is the declaration, "Thou art a God ready to forgive" (Neh. 9:17). "Who is a God like thee, pardoning iniquity . . . ?" (Mic. 7:18). "Our God . . . will abundantly pardon" (Isa. 55:7). From the beginning of his self-disclosure in the morning of the world's story to its climax in the person and work of Christ the Lord, God is revealed as the forgiving God.

With many words of promise and in many different ways in the Old Testament God made himself known as "ready to forgive." Sin with all its woes had barely entered the world when God declared that Satan, the inspirer of man's sad fall, would be brought to account. For the seed of the woman would bruise the serpent's head (Gen. 3:15). "It is full well known," says John Owen, "that the mystery of forgiveness is wrapt up in this one word of promise"; and that this "revelation of forgiveness with God, in this one promise, was the foundation of all the worship yielded to him by sinners for many generations."[31] Although the blood sacrifices of ancient leviticalism could not of themselves take away sin and allay the sting of conscience (see Heb. 10:1–2), they did speak of God's forgiveness of the worshiper and pointed forward to the certain grounds of that forgiveness—Christ's atoning sacrifice.

The reality of forgiveness in the Old Testament is thus rooted in what is there revealed of God's nature. The one grand affirmation concerning God in the earlier economy is that he is "good and forgiving" (Ps. 86:5). To the people of Israel, whom he chose as the recipients of his self-disclosure, he made himself known not as a stern and forbidding deity, but as "merciful and gracious, . . . keeping steadfast love for thousands, forgiving iniquity and transgression and sin" (Exod. 34:6–7). He is not one from whom forgiveness has to be wrenched either by purchase or bribe. Thus the psalmist can appeal for pardon of his great guilt "for thy name's sake, O LORD" (Ps. 25:11), and a prophet can make supplication for forgiveness on the ground of God's "great mercy" (Dan. 9:18–19). God's mercy and compassion (Ps. 78:38) and his

[31]Owen, *Forgiveness*, p. 130.

abundance of steadfast love (Ps. 86:5; cf. Isa. 55:7) are the grounds of his forgiveness. While God's justice might warrant the rejection and disownment of a sinner, God's love inspires him to forgive (Exod. 34:7; Neh. 9:16–17; Ps. 103:11–12; Mic. 7:18–22). Psalm 32 has been called a "Great Psalm of Forgiveness."[32] It opens with the exulting affirmation, "Blessed is he whose transgression is forgiven, whose sin is covered." Maclaren affirms, "One must have a dull ear not to hear the voice of personal experience in this Psalm. It throbs with emotion, and is a burst of rapture from a heart tasting the sweetness of the new joy of forgiveness."[33] Before God the psalmist acknowledges his iniquity and confesses his sin, and testifies that he is forgiven (v. 5). He has been pardoned, "eased of a burthen, a heavy burthen, like a load on the back, to make us stoop, or a load on the stomach, to make us sick, or a load on the spirits, that makes us sink."[34]

John Owen prefers to single out Psalm 130 as the great psalm of forgiveness. His classic volume *The Forgiveness of Sins* carries the subtitle *A Practical Exposition of Psalm 130*. Certainly throughout its eight short verses there is the ringing assurance that sin is forgivable. The early part of the psalm breathes the prayer of a soul conscious of its sin, and the latter part the peaceful confidence of one who has discovered the forgiving mercy of God. The psalmist is sure of God's "plenteous redemption," which is more abundant than all of Israel's iniquities (vv. 7–8). With Jehovah is steadfast love (v. 7); therefore there is forgiveness with him (v. 4). The addition "that thou mayest be feared" is unexpected and has puzzled commentators. But it is proper and intelligible. Forgiveness is a reality of God's goodness, while man's experience of forgiveness is the secret and source of all right regard for God. No one can truly reverence, love, and draw near to God with rapture, humility, and confidence except those who have come to the awareness and assurance of his forgiving mercy.

[32]C. Ryder Smith, *The Bible Doctrine of Salvation* (London: Epworth, 1941), p. 80.

[33]Alexander Maclaren, *The Book of Psalms*, The Expositor's Bible (London: Hodder & Stoughton, 1908), vol. 1, p. 302.

[34]Matthew Henry on Psalm 32.

So significant a place does the concept of forgiveness hold in the Old Testament that there are three specific words, as well as a number of graphic images, to convey the fact of God's rich pardon. Of the three words *sālach* (from the root *slch)* is the nearest equivalent of our term "forgive" (Exod. 34:9; Num. 14:19–20; 30:5; etc.). The word *nāsā,* which has the fundamental meaning of "to lift" or "to carry," occasionally bears the sense of the lifting off of a weight (i.e., the pardon of sin—Gen. 50:17; Exod. 10:17; etc.). In three instances the word *kāphar* has the sense of forgiveness (2 Chron. 30:18; Ps. 78:38; Jer. 18:23). Among the graphic images which convey the idea of forgiveness are descriptions of sin's being washed away (Ps. 51:2), removed (Ps. 103:12), cast behind God's back (Isa. 38:17), blotted out (Isa. 43:25), swept away like a cloud and like mist (Isa. 44:22), remembered no more (Jer. 31:34), and trodden under foot and cast into the depths of the sea (Mic. 7:19).

Profound and real, however, as was the awareness of forgiveness of sin in Old Testament times, this awareness was in a certain sense precarious, for it was easily undermined, if not for some altogether destroyed, by the onslaught of personal calamity. The nature of salvation in the Old Testament being tied in with animal sacrifice, and thus external rather than specifically personal, conditioned, in some measure, the understanding of forgiveness. Reversals such as disease or loss of goods the devout believer was inclined to interpret as evidence that God was no longer at peace with him. Adversity was regarded as divine judgment. God's treatment of the human individual was thought to reflect his true relation to him. Many of the psalms give voice to this view and reveal how personal misfortune shook confidence in the certainty of God's actual forgiveness. The presence of disaster, impending or actual, was read as a sign of God's displeasure and his casting off of those upon whom such trial had fallen, or, at least, as a sign that he had withdrawn his favor. Yet the eclipse of faith was never seen to be final or permanent, for even in the darkest night of the soul these same psalmists discovered, as did Job and the prophets, that God's love was steadfast and sure and would not let them go. The hope that God would turn towards them once more shone through like a beam of light through a chink in a drawn curtain. Although suffering and agony might cast a shadow over their pardon and acceptance, their struggling faith triumphed at length in the conviction of God's abiding presence. In the realization of pardon, even in the midst of what was thought of as the condemning judgment of misfortune, the saints of the Old Testament period proved and proclaimed that God's salvation is truly expressed and made real in the forgiveness of sins.

In the gospel of the New Testament, forgiveness is more surely stated and more firmly based. Indeed, according to P. T. Forsyth, "the forgiveness of sin is the foundation and genesis of Christianity; it is not an incident in it, nor in the Christian life."[35] The New Testament writers focus on forgiveness as the primary part in the scheme of God's salvation, and thus feature the concept as the distinctive of the Christian revelation. It has consequently been judged that it is this aspect of the evangelical proclamation which accounts for Christianity's early success in the world of competing religions. "It is a new element in a faith which tells, and Christianity overcame by means of its message of forgiveness in which it had no rivals."[36] The word of the gospel is founded upon this reality of God's forgiveness. In truth, "the whole of ethics rests on this article of the forgiveness of sin."[37]

The first reference (i.e., chronologically) in the New Testament to the subject of forgiveness comes in the Benedictus of Zechariah, which announces that John will be the forerunner of the Messiah and that his mission will be "to give knowledge of salvation to his people in the forgiveness of their sins" (Luke 1:77). So John the Baptist declared in his anticipatory message, "a baptism of repentance for the forgiveness of sins" (Mark 1:4; Luke 3:3).

The general New Testament expression for forgiveness—*aphiēmi*—has the sense of "to loose," "to send away," "to remit." In the one passage in the Fourth Gospel where *aphiēmi* carries the meaning of "forgive," the well-known

---

[35]Forsyth, *Positive Preaching*, p. 341.

[36]Mackintosh, *Christian Experience*, p. 21.

[37]Karl Barth, *The Heidelberg Catechism for Today* (London: Epworth, 1964), p. 87.

declaration of our Lord assuring his apostolic preachers the right to forgive sins through and in his name by the gospel, the English versions generally translate "to remit" (John 20:23). On the other hand, the word *aphiēmi* is commonly used in the Synoptic Gospels to denote forgiveness. Its appearance in the familiar petition of the Lord's Prayer, "Forgive us our debts" (Matt. 6:12), or "our sins" (Luke 11:4), when combined with the declaration of Matthew 6:14–15 and Mark 11:25, establishes God's willingness to forgive under certain conditions. The prayer of Jesus on the cross, "Father, forgive them," may be taken as assuring that sins of the most stupid horror are not outside the range of the divine forgiveness. Thus is declared God's readiness to forgive all sin, even that "against the Son of man," excepting only blasphemy against the Holy Spirit, which credits to the evil one what is truly and only of God (Matt. 12:32 and parallels). This surely is the one sin which puts a man beyond the reach of God's pardoning mercy. For to allow oneself to become so blinded and obtuse as to fail to recognize God at work is to commit an "eternal sin." It is to sin oneself into a position in which the awareness of what is good and of God is lost.

The opposite of sin is faith. In the commitment of faith a man discovers through God's grace the certainty of forgiveness. In the obduracy of sin a man may reject in despair the possibility of God's redemptive pardon. He may refuse faith —and to refuse faith is the ultimate sin. That is surely the sin against the Holy Spirit, when a man consciously and deliberately cuts himself off from God's holy forgiveness. For Christ declared that, "because they do not believe in me," it is the Spirit's work to convict the world of sin (John 16:8–9). It is not man's goodness, then, which is the contrary of sin, but faith: "Whatever is not of faith is sin" (Rom. 14:23).

The commentator F. Godet has this to say on the Lucan passage about the unforgivable sin against the Holy Spirit (12:10): "Jesus is ready to pardon in this world and the next indignity offered to his person; but an insult offered to goodness as such, and to the living principle in the heart of humanity, the Holy Spirit, the impious audacity of putting the holiness of his works to the account of the spirit of evil—that is what he calls blaspheming the Holy Spirit, and what he declares unpardonable."[38] In such a state a man may well declare, like Satan in Milton's *Paradise Lost,* "Myself am hell." Such a person has lost all spiritual sensitiveness and forfeited the power to repent. Having left no way open for the action of the Spirit, that individual has slipped into a position where even the forgiveness of God cannot reach.

With this one exception of the sin against the Holy Spirit, the New Testament consistently promises forgiveness for all our wrongs. Paul, for example, encourages the Colossian and Ephesian believers—although here his word is *charizomai*—with the assurance of their divine forgiveness through Christ (Col. 2:13; 3:13; Eph. 4:32). The First Epistle of John contains the promise that "if we confess our sins, he is faithful and just, and will forgive [*aphiēmi*] our sins and cleanse us from all unrighteousness" (1:9).

The noun *aphesis,* usually translated "remission," should be considered right along with the many instances of the verb *aphiēmi.* In Acts, where the noun form appears more frequently than in any other book, every occurrence is immediately followed by the genitive construction "of sins" (2:38; 5:31; 10:43; 13:38; 26:18). To both Jew and Gentile the gospel of forgiveness was proclaimed (13:38; 26:18). If it still be thought that the explicit references to forgiveness are comparatively few, it should be pointed out that they are nevertheless definite and clear enough to establish that the declaration of sin's forgiveness is an essential element of New Testament doctrine, if not indeed the very essence of the gospel itself. Thus does R. W. Dale assert, "To proclaim the remission of sins, as well as to make known the power and grace by which sinful men may recover the image of God, was one of the chief duties of the Apostles, and it is one of the chief duties of the Church in every age. To deny the possibility of remission, to deprecate its value, is to pervert the gospel of Christ."[39]

---

[38]F. Godet, *Commentary on St. Luke's Gospel,* trans. M. D. Cusin (Edinburgh: T. & T. Clark, n.d.), vol. 2, p. 93.

[39]R. W. Dale, *The Atonement* (London: The Congregational Union of England and Wales, 1902), p. 352.

3

Christ and Forgiveness

Forgiveness Divine and Human

Although the experience of forgiveness was a reality of which believers during the Old Testament economy were certainly aware, it was the view of the prophets that this forgiveness was based on and would be fully realized in a signal act of God designed to take place in the messianic age. In this they were, of course, right. For when the Messiah, Jesus of Nazareth, came, the message of divine forgiveness became absolute in him. Jesus was, contends Otto Borchert, "the first to recognize the power of forgiveness"—not "as something to be taken for granted, but always as something greatly wonderful."[1] Thus, while the general teaching of Jesus can be read as an elaboration of the Old Testament declaration of Psalm 86:5, that God is good and ready to forgive, Jesus gave forgiveness a new immediacy and fullness. In petition and parable, in prayer and proclamation, he made clear that God is surely willing to forgive. His coming brought a fuller disclosure of God, revealing the immeasurability of the forgiveness imparted by the heavenly Father.

In this regard the central petition of the Lord's Prayer, "And forgive us our sins, for we ourselves forgive every one

[1] Otto Borchert, *The Original Jesus*, trans. L. M. Stalker (London: Lutterworth, 1933), p. 368.

39

who is indebted to us" (Luke 11:4; cf. Matt. 6:12—"And forgive us our debts, As we also have forgiven our debtors"), is significant. The conjunction of "forgive us" and "as we have forgiven" does not put a limit on God's forgiveness, although it does indicate a close connection between his forgiveness of man and man's forgiveness of his fellows. In the declaration of Matthew 6:14–15, "For if you forgive men their trespasses, your heavenly Father also will forgive you; but if you do not forgive men their trespasses, neither will your Father forgive your trespasses," this relation is further emphasized. It is, then, only the one who forgives who can be forgiven. This is not, however, a case of the *lex talionis*, the law of retaliation. Rather, both this petition of the Lord's Prayer and this declaration of the prayer's Lord (Matt. 6:14–15) depict a God who is "forgiving with a sublimity and a universality of intention which displays all the characteristics of human pardon at its highest pitch; but in addition [there are] certain elements of Divine infinitude and wonder that open vistas into a new realm."[2]

It may seem but to garble a pious platitude to say that God's forgiveness cannot be less open and wholehearted than man's. For it is a deep and grand spiritual truth that the noblest manifestation of human forgiveness is no more than a pale shadow of the divine. The forgiveness of God is not for a moment, nor is it with measure. It partakes of his own everlastingness.

The connection between human forgiveness and the divine is, nonetheless, of vital spiritual moment: for those who would know divine forgiveness and for those who have received it. For there is "no relation to man without a relation to God, and no relation to God without relation to man, and it is only our relation to Jesus which provides our relation to man and to God."[3] As regards those who would know divine forgiveness, it is declared that God's forgiveness is open only to those who can forgive others. "And when you stand praying, if you have a grievance against anyone, forgive him, so that your Father in heaven may forgive you the wrongs you

[2]H. R. Mackintosh, *The Christian Experience of Forgiveness* (London: Nisbet, 1927), p. 31.

[3]Dietrich Bonhoeffer, *Ethics* (London: SCM, 1955), p. 192.

have done" (Mark 11:25, NEB). This, according to Jesus, is the one binding condition on those who would know the forgiveness of God. In truth, the forgiveness of God is believable only to the forgiving. For the one who shuts up his heart against all pleas for his forgiveness is certainly in no mood to understand or appreciate the holy pardon of God. An unforgiving spirit reveals an unrepentant heart, and divine forgiveness is withheld from unrepentant hearts. "Our forgiveness of others will not procure forgiveness for ourselves; but our not forgiving others proves that we ourselves are not forgiven."[4]

There are indeed some states of mind to which a man may give expression which render it impossible for him to receive anything of the Lord. There are those like the Pharisee in the temple (Luke 18:10–11) who so present themselves before God that they neither want nor will accept his divinest gift. "A man who cherishes hardness of heart towards those who have injured him so offends against the law of love that he cannot be received by the God of love, and cannot enjoy the restored relationship which he asks for in the Divine forgiveness, the whole significance of which is due to the supremacy of love."[5]

Not only, however, must those who would know the forgiveness of God evince a forgiving spirit, but even more must those who already have been forgiven display a forgiving attitude. It is the forgiven who can and who should forgive. "If your brother sins, rebuke him, and if he repents, forgive him; and if he sins against you seven times in the day, and turns to you seven times, and says, 'I repent,' you must forgive him" (Luke 17:3–4). Under the levitical law the righteous man was bidden to rebuke his neighbor and not "to bear sin because of him"; under the gospel the believing soul is charged to forgive the penitent wrongdoer, if by being forgiven he may be helped to a better and more godly life.

The truly grand word of the gospel to forgive others (Eph. 4:32; cf. Rom. 12:5) is not for the forgiven man simply a call to obey a divine injunction, but rather a call for an explosive

[4]John Owen, *The Forgiveness of Sin* (reprint, Grand Rapids: Baker, 1977), p. 209.

[5]W. T. Davison, "Forgiveness," in *Dictionary of Christ and the Gospels*, ed. J. Hastings (Edinburgh: T. & T. Clark, 1906), vol. 1, p. 618.

outgoing of the heart which knows the forgiveness of God in Christ. The experience of forgiveness must surely stir the believer not only with readiness to forgive, but with eagerness to do so. And such forgiveness has no limit, either as regards the number of times—until seventy times seven—or the persons to be forgiven—all men, even including enemies. By such forgiveness the pardoned sinner himself participates in God's own attitude to all sinners and makes credible to the world the gospel of forgiveness. For "no grace, no duty, no ornament of the mind is in itself so lovely, so praiseworthy or so useful to mankind, as are meekness and readiness to forgive."[6]

The church as the community of the forgiven stands—or at any rate should stand—before the world as the living embodiment of forgiveness, both human and divine. It is, in fact, in the context of mutual forgiveness as demonstrated within the Christian fellowship that God's forgiveness of sinners is the most effectually proclaimed. Where the church is characterized by disharmony, wrangling, and bitterness the pronouncement of reconciliation and peace with the God who is love must sound hollow. Only when the atmosphere of the Christian community is warm with brotherhood does the gospel ring true. This is the meaning of the declaration of Christ recorded in the Fourth Gospel: "If you forgive the sins of any, they are forgiven; if you retain the sins of any, they are retained" (John 20:23). The "notion which afterwards blossomed or faded into the belief that the church as an hierarchical institution has authority to admit or to exclude from the benefits of salvation, in this life and the next," can be set aside.[7] Nonetheless, the words of John 20:23 do contain a deep spiritual lesson which needs constantly to be learned and constantly to be lived by the church. The efforts which a Christian man who has succumbed to some gross evil is making to begin again will be greatly influenced by the attitude held towards him by his fellow believers. If they withdraw, scorn him, and become censorious, he will be discouraged. It is not likely that he will speedily and spontaneously seek the renewing forgiveness of a loving heavenly

[6]Owen, *Forgiveness*, p. 209.
[7]Mackintosh, *Christian Experience*, p. 283.

Father. Where there are none, or few, to seek him out and assure him of reconciliation in the fellowship of those who claim to be right with God, he may come to believe that he is also beyond the range of God's pardon. On the other hand, should he find that the Christian community, while frankly recognizing his fall, still welcomes him with full forgiveness, he will consider that no limit can be set to the re-creating tenderness with which God's loving forgiveness may once again flood and overflow his heart.

Making the point that the pronouns of John 20:23 are unemphatic, B. F. Westcott goes on to insist that the power of absolution is not confined to a particular class. "The commission therefore must be regarded properly as the commission of the Christian society and not as that of the Christian ministry. (Comp. Matt. v. 13, 14.) The great mystery of the world, absolutely insoluble by thought, is that of sin; the mission of Christ was to bring salvation from sin, and the work of His Church is to apply to all that which he has gained."[8] A high responsibility thus rests with the Christian community in the matter of forgiveness. By not forgiving, the church can bind a man to his sinful past; by forgiving, on the other hand, the church can loose him from it, helping him towards seeking renewal of peace with God in the forgiveness of his sins. Indeed, the "only forgiveness Jesus recognizes is that which makes the forgiven heart the home of the love which forgives."[9]

Christ's Teaching: The Father's Willingness to Forgive

Forgiveness has a central place in Christianity only because of Jesus. It is because of him that forgiveness is fully credible. Because of his presence in the world, the message and manner of divine forgiveness have become a redemptive and radiant actuality. By Jesus forgiveness was proclaimed and in Jesus it is pronounced. Prominent in his teaching is the assurance of the Father's readiness to forgive. And he, "like

[8] B. F. Westcott, *The Gospel According to St. John* (London: John Murray, 1908), p. 295.

[9] James Denney, *The Christian Doctrine of Reconciliation* (London: Hodder & Stoughton, 1918), p. 137.

the more 'evangelical' Old Testament prophets, represents forgiveness as a pure act of grace on the part of God, who on the repentance of the sinner receives him graciously and pardons his transgression in the sense of replacing the offender in his former relation of acceptance and favour."[10] According to the teaching of Jesus forgiveness is the foundation of the kingdom of God. Jesus notes that this outpouring of the divine goodwill is the beginning of the kingdom's blessings; thus he exalts forgiveness into a principle which lifts man out of his sin and shame to be a child and citizen of the realm of God.

The central petition of the Lord's Prayer assures us that it is not futile to ask the heavenly Father for forgiveness. In this connection Jesus' parable of the prodigal son (Luke 15:11–32) teaches that forgiveness is full and free. F. Godet, one of the best of the New Testament expositors, has commented on the Father's welcome of the younger brother (vv. 20b–24): "Free pardon, entire restoration, the joys of adoption,—such are the contents of these verses. The heart of God overflows in the sayings of Jesus. Every word vibrates with emotion, at once the tenderest and the holiest. The father never seems to have given up waiting for his son; perceiving him from afar, he runs to meet him. God discerns the faintest sign after good which breaks forth in a wanderer's heart; and from the moment this heart takes a step towards Him, He takes ten to meet it, striving to show it something of His love."[11]

There is, to be sure, no mention in the parable of the grounds on which the returning prodigal was forgiven. The purpose of the tale, however, is manifestly to declare that forgiveness for wrongdoing is available for all who, confessing their need of forgiveness, return to their Father's home. There is indeed no cross in the story, except in the aching heart of the father. This does not mean, however, as Adolf von Harnack supposed, that the gospel of the Synoptics is simply that of a kindly heavenly Father who forgives sin with an unholy ease, for in other places and in other ways the New Testament makes clear that in forgiveness God's justice is

[10]Davison, "Forgiveness," p. 616.

[11]F. Godet, *Commentary on St. Luke's Gospel*, trans. M. D. Cusin (Edinburgh: T. & T. Clark, n. d.), vol. 2, pp. 153–54.

never compromised by his goodness, nor his holiness by his love. In the story Jesus was emphasizing one aspect of the truth which the religion of his time had woefully obscured, namely, that there is ready forgiveness with God for the sinner who returns. This was a word sorely needed. For the scribes and Pharisees had left the people of the land with little hope of acceptance by God, while to the outcast Gentiles they gave virtually no hope at all. The lesson emphatically taught by Jesus in the story of the returning prodigal is that the divine forgiveness is full and free. "The son did not buy his forgiveness, nor did anybody buy it for him. Nothing he could do could ever repay it. His father forgave him because he was his father and loved him with an indefeasible love, more strong and wonderful than all his sins."[12]

Christ's Pronouncement of Forgiveness

There was, however, something even more significant in Jesus' relation to forgiveness. For not only did he teach that God is willing to forgive, but he also asserted his own right to pronounce the sinner forgiven. Thus he himself "declared, bestowed, and embodied forgiveness."[13]

No prophet ever took to himself the role of forgiving men their sins. But to the paralytic man (Matt. 9:1–8; cf. Mark 2:1–12; Luke 5:17–26) Jesus declared forgiveness in his own name. Jesus pardoned the paralytic in a single comprehensive sentence: "Your sins are forgiven you." For, says C. H. Spurgeon in a powerful sermon on the passage, "Christ's voice had such almighty power about it that it needed not to utter many words. There was no long lesson for the poor man to repeat, there was no intricate problem for him to work out in his mind. The Master said all that was required in that one sentence, 'Thy sins are forgiven thee.'"[14] And Helmut Thielicke, echoing these words of Spurgeon, declares that when Jesus "met a guilty man, he did not preach a sermon or deliver a lecture on the theme that God is a Judge before

[12]Denney, *Christian Doctrine*, p. 132.
[13]Ibid., p. 131.
[14]C. H. Spurgeon, *The Miracles of Our Lord* (London: Hodder & Stoughton, 1901), vol. 2, p. 281.

whom he must perish, but that God is also merciful and will perhaps justify him in grace if he will take up a right attitude towards him. No, he tells a man directly and authoritatively: 'Your sins are forgiven.' And as he says this the man knows that his chains fall off, that he can stand up and go away a new creature. When Jesus speaks we have more than a word; we have an enactment, a creative deed which makes things new.''[15]

Christ's word is an action; he speaks and it is done. His word to the paralytic was not just the expression of a hope, a wish, a possibility. He declared the man's sins forgiven; and forgiven they were, really, truly, actually. "The absolving words are not *optative*, no mere desire that it might be, but *declaratory* that so it was; the man's sins *were* forgiven. Nor yet were they declaratory only of something which passed in the mind and intention of God; but, even as the words were spoken, there was shed abroad in his heart the sense of forgiveness and reconciliation with God."[16]

Those nearby who heard Christ's stirring affirmation of the man's forgiveness wondered and praised God, acknowledging that some unprecedented and superhuman power had been entrusted to a son of man. Jesus' claim, however, that as the Son of man the authority was his to forgive sin provoked the Pharisees. They first reasoned, "Who can forgive sins but God alone?" and, of course, they reasoned rightly, knowing the Scriptures and the power of God. For "to the Lord our God belong mercies and forgiveness, though we have rebelled against him" (Dan. 9:9, KJV). They then concluded that Jesus spoke blasphemy by asserting that as Son of man he had authority to forgive sins; in this case they did not know the Scriptures and the power of God, and so they arrived at a wrong conclusion. Pardon is indeed a supernatural act; it is altogether a divine word. Thus, if Christ were only a man, then they were right to declare him a blasphemer. But they did not consider that, in his penetrating to the man's inner and more fundamental need, Jesus showed that he "knew

[15]Helmut Thielicke, *A Thielicke Trilogy* (Grand Rapids: Baker, 1980), pp. 129–30.

[16]R. C. Trench, *Notes on the Miracles of Our Lord* (London: Kegan Paul, Trench, 1886), p. 218.

what was in man" (John 2:25). Jesus discerned the thoughts and intents of the heart (Heb. 4:12) and thereby revealed himself as Godlike and divine (see 1 Sam. 16:7; 1 Kings 8:39; 1 Chron. 28:9; 2 Chron. 6:30; Prov. 15:11; Jer. 17:10; Ezek. 11:5). The Pharisees did not see in Jesus the "expression of God's forgiveness," nor perceive in him "as nowhere else the nearness of God."[17]

There is an implied antithesis between authority "on earth" and authority "in heaven" (see Matt. 16:19; 8:18). Yet as Son of man on earth Jesus was also at once from heaven (John 3:13, 31, etc.) and in heaven (John 3:13, KJV; cf. 6:62; 17:5, 24). Thus the words he spoke and the works he did were no less those of the Father: they were the words and works of God. Consequently, in declaring forgiveness, "Jesus dealt with the palsied man in a truly royal and divine way."[18]

Jesus confronted his critics with the challenging question, "Which is easier, to say, 'Your sins are forgiven,' or to say, 'Rise and walk'?" They might suppose that it was easier to *say*, "Your sins are forgiven." For what proof could there be of such a transaction being actualized in the inner and hidden recesses of a human life? It must surely be harder to say, "Rise and walk," and then to effect this command. So Jesus spoke the word, and the limbs of the paralytic man came to immediate use as a demonstration of Christ's power and right to do what in the nature of the case lay outside the region of visible proof. By his taking up his bed and walking away with sure foot and steady step, the man gave visible demonstration of his forgiveness. "The material miracle, therefore, is worked," says Jerome in his Commentary on Matthew, "to prove the spiritual."

In this instance Jesus put his spiritual authority to forgive in the foreground of his ministry and publicly proclaimed it, while on other occasions he privately and quietly wrought forgiveness in the souls of those who experienced his healing touch. The paralytic and those about him heard Jesus' word of forgiveness first. Thus Jesus focused the minds of all on the reality of forgiveness, and then he performed the physical

---

[17]W. Herrmann, *Communion of the Christian with God*, trans. J. Sandys Stanyon (Philadelphia: Fortress, 1971), p. 141.

[18]Spurgeon, *Miracles*, pp. 282–83.

cure as the seal and authentication of the man's actual pardon. "He manifested that his object in doing these works in men's bodies," says Augustine of Hippo, "was that he might be believed to set free the souls of sinners by his remission; in other words that by the exercise of his visible authority he might gain belief in his invisible authority."[19]

Akin in significance to the story of the paralytic man is that of the sinful woman (Luke 7:36–50). Jesus assured her of a full forgiveness. When Simon, in whose house Jesus was a guest, protested at the presence of a "sinner" and at Jesus' acceptance of her lavish outpouring of love, Jesus replied, "Her sins, which are many, are forgiven, for she loved much"(v. 47). Whether the woman had met Jesus before this incident in Simon's house is not certain. Herrmann thinks she had not. Godet, however, affirms that somehow, somewhere, there must have been a previous encounter, whether "in a private interview, or through one of those looks of Jesus which for broken hearts were like a ray of heaven." Already, according to Godet, she had tasted the joy of salvation so that the perfume she brought was an emblem of her ardent gratitude for this unspeakable gift. We need not take sides on the issue, for the significant thing in the story is Jesus' absolute remission of the woman's many sins. In his *Edifying Discourses* Søren Kierkegaard declares this "one thing was absolutely important to her; to find forgiveness."[20] There was nothing the woman did, or could do, to procure that forgiveness; nothing could secure it for her but to hear it from the lips of Christ. From him alone could she rejoice in the reassuring word of pardon. Throughout, the woman herself said not a word; indeed she made no plea at all. She merely stood or maybe knelt before the Lord; that was her way of confession, her manner of expressing her great need. "So she goes home again—a dumb person in the whole scene. Who would guess what this expedition meant to her, this expedition when she went thither in sin and sorrow, and came home with forgiveness and joy?"[21]

[19]Quoted in Trench, *Notes*, p. 223.
[20]Søren Kierkegaard, *Training in Christianity*, trans. Walter Lowrie (London: Oxford University, 1941), p. 265 (and repeated on p. 266).
[21]Ibid., p. 268.

The woman may not have heard the conversation between Jesus and Simon. Yet one word she did hear; one word about her and for her. "Her sins, which are many, are forgiven." That she did hear and know. It may be, as Kierkegaard believes, that she did not hear the rest of the sentence—"for she loved much." For on hearing the word of forgiveness she probably turned to get hold of her perfume vessel; the following words of Jesus might then have been lost to her. To have heard his word of forgiveness was enough! She knew too well in herself that it was not her love that had called out so divine a wonder as to bring her a full discharge from her many sins. "Hence," says Kierkegaard, "I assume that she did not hear [the rest of the sentence], or perhaps she heard it but heard amiss, so that she thought [Jesus] said, 'Because He loved much,' so that what was said had reference to His infinite love, that *because* it was so infinite, therefore her many sins were forgiven her, which she could so perfectly well understand, for it was as if she herself had said so."[22]

The only way to account for what Jesus describes as the woman's generous love is to view it as her response to God's infinite love for her. She loved because she knew God loved her first and had forgiven her. The "for" or "because" (Greek *hoti*) in verse 47 is not to be interpreted, then, as meaning that she was forgiven because she loved much. Rather, the force of the word is that the guests in Simon's house could be assured that she had been forgiven much, for they saw the result—her lavish outpouring of love. Her acceptance and divine forgiveness had taken place before her grateful love was manifested. "In light of the indignation of the Pharisee in whose home this took place, one can conclude that those who lack forgiveness have little love to give."[23] The woman found in Jesus the security and guarantee of an astonishing kindness. The forgiveness which he pronounced, and which had come to her soul, she knew was not bought by her gift, nor was it compelled by her display of emotion. It was altogether of him, freely and fully bestowed without price. Note also that Jesus did not keep her in suspense, either by making her

[22]Ibid.

[23]Donald G. Bloesch, *Essentials of Evangelical Theology* (San Francisco: Harper & Row, 1978), vol. 1, p. 184.

chronicle all the sordid details of her past and then wait for him to fully consider her case, or by putting her on probation to see if she was truly sorry for her past. The fact that she was there—that she had come to him—was enough. He did not upbraid her for her waywardness, nor utter thundering accusations against her. For a bruised reed he will not break, and the smoking flax he will not quench.

Jesus saw in the woman a hope, a longing, a desire which had driven her to him as someone (indeed, the only one) both willing and able to give her at once a new heart and a new start. As she heard his word that her many sins were forgiven, she knew of a certainty she had received from him divine pardon.

And that is surely the lesson writ large in the story. Nowhere, it may be noted, is the name of God mentioned. Yet God is there present in every action and reaction of Jesus. Because of him the woman was sure of God's own pardon of her many sins. In the presence of Jesus she felt the security of God's goodness and kindness. In Simon's house she came to realize that there was something divinely new and wondrous abroad in the world. For in Jesus there was an element which tippèd the balance against despair, an element which, it is clear, cannot be described simply in terms of being something mysterious and unaccountable. Says Thielicke emphatically, "She sees the divine element in Jesus before others, even before those for whom religion is a vocation, and she does so because she is led to the frontier where alone she can go no further and knows herself to be lost."[24] She sees in him that "essential, distinctive and most fundamental quality of God which the New Testament calls love."[25] Jesus was "this woman's Saviour because through His attitude she once for all knew that God was on her side, and was there and then receiving her as His child. Thus there was laid down at the foundation of her life that initial certainty of His pardoning love which opened to her the gates of righteousness."[26]

The French philosopher Joseph de Maistre relates a story of an ascetic who has a vision in which, as in the story of Job,

[24]Thielicke, *Trilogy*, p. 144.
[25]Mackintosh, *Christian Experience*, p. 94.
[26]Ibid.

Satan stands before the throne of God. The saint overhears the evil spirit protest against God's verdict of condemnation. "Why must I be damned," he asks, "who have sinned but once, and yet God, you are saving thousands whose offenses are so much more?" To his enquiry, he receives God's answer, "Have you but once asked pardon?" This is the truth of the matter. No one will be lost who appeals for God's forgiveness. Those who will not seek his mercy will not have it.

The first heralds of the good news of God's salvation went forth into the world with the ringing certainty of divine forgiveness in Christ for all who would heed and respond in faith. God's forgiveness of man "for Christ's sake" was their message (Eph. 4:32; Col. 3:13). Such forgiveness, they proclaimed, becomes a personal experience "in Christ" (Eph. 1:7; Col. 1:14); and in Christ's name it is assured (1 John 1:9). Thus the inspired writers of the New Testament and the first preachers of its gospel set forth Christ as the one in whom God's grace in free and full forgiveness is alone mediated. They did not "propose this way of forgiveness as the best and most pleasant, but as the only way. There is no other name but that of Christ; no other way but this of forgiveness."[27]

The forgiveness of sins is, then, as Kierkegaard says, the greatest renewal Christianity has brought to the world. 'Thy sins are forgiven thee' (Luke 7:48), that is the cry of encouragement of the Christians one to another; with this cry Christianity spread over the world; by these words it is recognized as a race apart, a separate nation."[28]

Christians are a people divinely forgiven; therefore they are, and therefore they must be, a people who forgive divinely.

[27]Owen, *Forgiveness*, p. 250.
[28]Kierkegaard, *Concluding Unscientific Postscript*, trans. David Swenson and Walter Lowrie (Princeton, N.J.: Princeton University, 1944), p. 95.

4

Grace and Forgiveness

The Definition of Grace

As divine pardon is the heart of the gospel, so the word of God's forgiveness is central in the Christian doctrine of grace. For, to be precise, according to Karl Barth, "grace is the forgiveness of sins."[1] Because God's love goes forth in mercy there is forgiveness with him; "infinite goodness and grace [are] the soil wherein forgiveness grows."[2] This word of grace is, then, the theme of the gospel. The couplet of questions in the refrain in Samuel Davies's hymn "Great God of Wonders!" expresses the almost unbelievable wonder of God's pardoning grace at work in the lives of those whom he forgives:

> Who is a pard'ning God like thee?
> Or who has grace so rich and free?

The answer to both questions is, of course, No one. There is none like God who pardons all iniquity (Ps. 103:3). None other than he is revealed as "the God of all grace" (1 Peter

[1]Karl Barth, *Credo* (London: Hodder & Stoughton, 1936), p. 154.
[2]John Owen, *The Forgiveness of Sin* (reprint, Grand Rapids: Baker, 1977), p. 90.

5:10), extending to sinners "its immeasurable riches" (Eph. 2:7) in the forgiveness of sins (Eph. 1:7). Barth can well claim that "grace is, then, the deepest and divinest word of the gospel. It opens a window to that which is deepest and divinest in God himself; that reality of God which disposes him to forgive sinners. To speak of grace is in truth to speak of God. Grace is then but another way of saying, gospel. For everything, absolutely everything, and to the last degree, is determined and conditioned by the fact that forgiveness of sins is gifted to man, and received by him as a gift."[3]

Not only is man forgiven on the basis of grace; he is also kept in the assurance of that forgiveness by grace. "If it is the grace of God that sets a man's feet at the entrance of the path-way of faith, it is equally the grace of God that enables him to continue and complete that path-way."[4] It is grace from first to last—and all the way in between. It is all of grace. "Grace there is my every debt to pay." In grace God does all that becomes him as the forgiving God. To forgive is part of his nature. This affirmation does not, however, lend support to the impertinent remark of Heinrich Heine, who said on his deathbed, "God will forgive—that's his business [*c'est son métier*]." For while God does and will forgive with ready grace, his forgiveness is not something he must dispense as by some ineluctable necessity. There is no *must* or inflexible causality in God's forgiveness, none save that of his kindness and goodness. His grace alone engenders his pardon. Thus it is that "without compulsion from outside or any necessity, but purely from the impulse of love, God seeks to save those whom there is no reason to save."[5] This is what is meant by grace: it is the unmerited favor of God, the outgoing of his love in compassion for sinful man. God's grace is his holy love in action, which seeks and saves those who are lost.

Yet God's forgiveness is not a sort of kindly general amnesty which covers all. From man's side it is there for "whoso-

[3]Barth, *Credo*, p. 153.

[4]F. F. Bruce, *The Epistle of Paul to the Romans: An Introduction and Commentary* (Grand Rapids: Eerdmans, 1963), p. 365.

[5]Tahashi Fugi, *Collected Works*, vol. 3, p. 490; quoted in Carl Michalson, *Japanese Contributions to Christian Theology* (Philadelphia: Westminster, 1960), p. 30.

ever will," while from God's side it is for whom he wills. In the last reckoning, then, forgiveness is open only to the forgivable. Thus, to say that we are saved by God's grace, which is free to all, does not mean that all are forgiven. Rather, "to say that we are saved by grace, is to say that we are saved both without merit on our own part, and without necessity on the part of God."[6] John Wesley struck the right note at the opening of his famous sermon on free grace:

> The Grace or Love of God, whence cometh our salvation, is free in all, and free for all.
> It is free in all to whom it is given. It does not depend on any power or merit in man; no, not in any degree, neither in whole, nor in part. It does not, in any case, depend either on the good works or righteousness of the receiver: not on anything he has done, or anything he is. It does not depend on his endeavours. It does not depend on his good tempers, or good desires, or good purposes and intentions. For all these flow from the grace of God: they are the streams only, not the fountain. They are the fruits of free grace, and not the root. They are not the cause, but the effects of it. Whatever good is in man, or is done by man, God is the author and doer of it. Thus in his grace free to all, that is, no way depending on any power, or merit in man; but on God alone, who freely gave us his own son, and "with him freely giveth us all things."[7]

In every act of God's forgiveness the motive and mainspring is his grace. Thus the forgiveness of our sins is according to the riches of his grace (Eph. 1:7). As sinners—and all have sinned (Rom. 3:23)—we have no right to expect from God anything but everlasting destruction on account of our great evil and grievous rebellion. "We can only claim from Him justice—and justice, for us, means certain condemnation. God does not owe it to anyone to stop justice taking its course. He is not obliged to pity and pardon; if He does so it is an act done, as we say, 'of His own free will,' and nobody forces His hand. 'It does not depend on man's will or effort,

[6]A. H. Strong, *Systematic Theology* (New York: A. C. Armstrong, 1889), p. 282.

[7]John Wesley, *The Works of John Wesley* (London: Printed at the Conference-Office, City Road, 1809), vol. 6, pp. 408–9.

but on God's mercy' (Romans 9:16, NEB). Grace is free, in the sense of being self-originated, and of proceeding from One who was free not to be gracious."[8]

So foundational is God's grace *(charis)* to his forgiveness of sins that the apostle Paul, in seeking a Greek word to express God's forgiveness, chose one which unmistakably features the concept of God's grace. Paul took over the word *charizomai*, which was in general use with the meaning of "to bestow" or "to give," and promoted it to do service for the Christian understanding of pardon. As pardon for sin was seen to be the gift of God, a divine and gracious boon, it was not unnatural that such a verb, which in everyday parlance meant simply "to give," should come to have the sense of "to forgive." "What seems to have led Paul to develop this verb was his consciousness of the divine grace in pardon. When he thought, 'God gives,' he instinctively thought, 'God forgives.'"[9] Etymologically *charizomai* is a word without religious or moral reference. But Paul brought it into the spiritual sphere and there employed it to express God's forgiveness, which was for the apostle a signal evidence of God's grace. God has "forgiven us all our trespasses," he tells the Colossians (Col. 2:13). The verse begins by noting the sins of the Colossians ("And you, who were dead in trespasses"), and it ends with Paul's including himself among them as having been forgiven ("God . . . having forgiven us all our trespasses"). His own experience taught Paul that God gives and God forgives, that his forgiving is his giving, and that such giving and forgiving is his grace. Thus God's grace is "sufficient" (2 Cor. 12:9); it is "enough" *(Phillips)*; it is "all you need" (NEB). Paul was overwhelmed by God's favor, and so he proclaimed "the gospel of the grace of God" (Acts 20:24) as "the word of his grace" (Acts 20:32) which assures God's forgiveness *(charizomai)* for Christ's sake (Eph. 4:32). In grace, then, does God's forgiveness come to man in reconciling pardon.

Grace is the divine order in which God's love reigns as forgiving mercy, and in which there is the firm assurance of God's utmost pardon of man's utmost sin. "Pardon flows

[8]J. I. Packer, *Knowing God* (London: Hodder & Stoughton, 1973), p. 146.

[9]James Moffatt, *Grace in the New Testament* (London: Hodder & Stoughton, 1931), p. 103.

immediately from a sovereign act of free grace. This free purpose of God's will and grace, for the pardoning of sinners, is indeed that which is principally intended, when we say, 'There is forgiveness with him'; that is, he is pleased to forgive; and so to do is agreeable with his nature."[10] What, then, is meant by the grace of God? Definitions abound in evangelical theology, all of which stress its nature as a gift grounded in the goodwill of God towards man. According to B. B. Warfield, grace is "God's sovereign favour for the ill-deserving."[11] Louis Berkhof conceives of grace as an attribute of the divine perfection displayed in "God's free, sovereign, undeserved favour or love towards man, in his state of sin and guilt, which manifests itself in the forgiveness of sin and deliverance from its penalty."[12]

The Nature of Grace: Personal and Unmeasurable

The general term used to denote God's grace to man, of which forgiveness is the central reality, is *salvation*. Thus the New Testament affirms that it is "the grace of God that bringeth salvation" (Titus 2:11, KJV), for "by grace you have been saved" (Eph. 2:8). Such grace is not, however, to be interpreted as an impersonal or abstract entity. By grace indeed we are saved, but this grace is no mysterious semiphysical substance or magical force communicated by a distant God through sacramental channels or priestly declarations. "We live in a world of beings, and God acts towards us not as impersonal force but as a fully personal activity directed impartially towards all men."[13] In salvation God himself is present in the outgoing of pure love in an absolute pardon which brings to the sinner reconciliation with God and the privilege of full sonship.

It is of the first importance to conceive of grace in terms of personal relationship. Unnecessary difficulties have been im-

[10]Owen, *Forgiveness*, p. 93.

[11]B. B. Warfield, *Selected Works of Benjamin B. Warfield*, ed. John E. Meeter (Nutley, N.J.: Presbyterian and Reformed, 1973), vol. 2, p. 427.

[12]Louis Berkhof, *Systematic Theology* (London: Banner of Truth, 1958), p. 427.

[13]E. B. Redlich, *The Forgiveness of Sins* (Edinburgh: T. & T. Clark, 1937), p. 119.

ported by conceiving of it as a sort of "sub-personal something given by God to work on its own, as a doctor may give a
patient a bottle of medicine to be taken three times a day
after meals."[14] Such a *"tertium quid* theory of grace," as
Lindsay Dewar refers to it, introduces a kind of third entity
between the soul and God.[15] The question then arises as to
whether it is to be assigned to God or man. If one assigns it to
man, as Pelagius does, then how can it be said that salvation
is the gift of God? If one assigns it to God absolutely, as
Augustine does, then what becomes of man's freedom? To
escape the dilemma all sorts of "grace" have had to be
distinguished and all sorts of compromises concerning the
relative contributions of God and man resorted to.

Some conceive of grace as a mechanistic force; others view
it as something like a material fluid. Those who think of it as a
force are led to raise such questions as, Is grace "irresistible"? And in attempting to answer that question there is
formed in the mind an idea of a cause-and-effect sequence
drawn from the physical world. The stress here is totally on
the omnipotence of God conceived of as an arbitrary sover-
eignty divorced altogether from love. On the other hand, the
view of grace as a kind of fluid leads at once to the notion that
the efficacy of the sacraments comes *ex opere operato.* Then
begin all those learned discussions and disquisitions of sacramental theology with their assurance that some sort of
infusion takes place at the subconscious level. With both
views (grace as a force or a fluid) there is danger of obscuring
the essential note of grace as God's love in action. And love
most surely operates within terms of conscious personal
relationships. Grace does not prevail the more impersonal it
is; rather it succeeds because it is most intimately personal.

Most of us have experienced a personal relationship that
has benefited us and influenced us greatly. We may not fully
understand how it affected us, but there is no question that
the personal help offered by another enabled us to will and to
do what we could not have willed or done on our own. Many a
man has reason to be grateful that through someone else's

[14]Leonard Hodgson, *For Faith and Freedom* (Oxford: Blackwell, 1956), vol.
2, p. 149.
     [15]Lindsay Dewar, *Magic and Grace* (London: SPCK, 1929), p. 115.

emancipating influence he has achieved the otherwise impossible. With gratitude he has testified that "but for So-and-so coming into my life I could never have been what I am or have done what I have done." There is, of course, always the danger that such influence may become so strong as to obliterate our active responsiveness and turn us into puppets of another's pleasure. But when it comes to God's dealings with man, no such danger exists. Israel was not steamrollered out of Egypt. They were awakened to responsiveness. God most surely can work upon us in so perfect a manner that out of bondage we come to respond in faith to his gracious influence. God's grace will most certainly triumph in those in whom he works, bringing them to faith and freedom in the experience of forgiveness. For the grace of God is nothing other than the triumphant love of the saving Christ.[16]

Grace is, then, the divine love in action, operating within a personal relationship. This is the truth about grace, fundamental in the biblical revelation, to which Christian experience gives fullest attestation. That God treats the sinner graciously and forgives sin outright without insisting first on any guarantees of better conduct is the very heart of the gospel. And in our being forgiven and brought into a new standing and status before God we come to experience the intensely personal nature of God's grace and loving mercy.

In addition to being personal, God's grace is unmeasurable. The love of God for bankrupt humanity cannot be qualified. It is not a love which merely transcends human pity and affection. It is a love unique in method and manner, a love which has entered the tragic realities of human life, sounding its depths and marking our condition. It is a love which takes full account of the fundamental reality of human sinfulness and deals with it in holy grace, forgiving it radically and effectively. "It is love in action, working for the sinner's salvation. It is not just any sort of love, but the strong pure love of God Himself. It is an overflowing love that pours itself out in streams of mercy to the unworthy; it is a love that goes to all lengths, that gives to the uttermost and exceeds all the excesses of sin (Rom. 5:20). Contrasted with the 'wages of sin,'

---

[16]Some statements in this section are based on portions of my *I and He* (London: Epworth, 1966), pp. 93–94.

it is 'the gift of God' (Rom. 6:23)."[17] Such is the love that saves, the love that forgives. It is all of grace, and what is of grace is altogether *gratis*.

God's grace is far greater and more powerful than the original sinful nature of man; and even when the added stains of our sinful acts are also taken into account, his grace is still far greater. "Where sin increased, grace abounded all the more" (Rom. 5:20). Grace is not, however, to be thought of as a quality measured out in proportion to the number of a person's actual sins. All of us are equally sinners and stand in need of the same grace. "Grace is never exercised by God by marking up what may be lacking in the life and character of a sinner. In such a case, much sinfulness would call for much greater grace, and little sinfulness would call for little grace."[18] God's grace, however, unlike man's, cannot be measured quantitatively. Grace is not a matter of mathematics. The forgiveness of a sinner is an act of God's free favor; it is, equally for all, nothing less than a full display of God's unmeasurable love. To suppose that there is a correlation between, on one hand, the number and overtness of one's sins and, on the other, the amount of forgiveness required is to misunderstand totally the nature and effects of grace and to run the danger of "insulting the very Spirit of Grace" (Heb. 10:29, *Phillips*).

Paul's Gospel of Grace and Forgiveness

It is not our purpose here to detail the biblical doctrine of grace.[19] However, something must be said on that aspect of it which concerns forgiveness. For while it is rightly observed that pardon "is not the whole doctrine of grace," it is still true that it is "the heart of the gospel."[20]

Christianity, it has been said, was the first religion to make "grace" a leading term. This is due in the main to Paul's prominent use of the word. Donald Bloesch declares that Paul

---

[17]E. F. Kevan, *Salvation* (Grand Rapids: Baker, 1963), p. 29.
[18]Lewis Sperry Chafer, *Grace* (Grand Rapids: Zondervan, n.d.), p. 5.
[19]See my *Salvation* (Westchester, Ill.: Crossway, 1982), chap. 11.
[20]Packer, *Knowing God*, p. 149.

is "the chief theologian of grace in the New Testament."[21] Yet grace for Paul was not simply a theology but his gospel. For the apostle was no mere academic theologian sitting in isolated seclusion, speculating on how God might deal with fallen man. Paul's "word of grace" is for the open road, not for the secluded study. It is a message for man in his sinning and living; it is good news of God, impossible for any man, even for a man of Paul's mind and heart, to have concocted or dreamed up. Paul's gospel of the grace of God is

> not a statement, nor a doctrine, nor a scheme, on man's side; nor an offer, a promise, or a book, on God's side. It is an act and a power: it is God's *act* of redemption before it is man's message of it. It is an eternal, perennial act of God in Christ, repeating itself within each declaration of it. Only as a Gospel done by God is it a Gospel spoken by man. It is a revelation only because it was first of all a reconciliation. It was a work that redeemed us into the power of understanding its own word. It is an objective power, a historic act and perennial energy of the holy love of God in Christ; decisive for humanity in time and eternity; and altering for ever the whole relation of the soul to God, as it may be rejected or believed. The gift of God's grace was, and is, His work of Gospel.[22]

Paul did not invent the word *grace*. It was long in use in Greek literature with many nuances of meaning, and the Septuagint had made the term *charis* do duty for such Hebrew ideas as "favor" (*hēn*) and "mercy" (*hesed*). But not even "the higher conception of the divine *hesed* or mercy is able in Judaism to achieve the place occupied by *charis* in Christianity."[23] As Paul, under the Holy Spirit's inspiration, reflected on his encounter with the risen Christ on the Damascus road, there were forced to his mind the two basic ideas which unite in the word *charis:* that the saving initiative is with God, and that any claim to human merit is totally

[21]Donald G. Bloesch, *Essentials of Evangelical Theology* (San Francisco: Harper & Row, 1978), vol. 1, p. 182.

[22]P. T. Forsyth, *Positive Preaching and the Modern Mind* (London: Hodder & Stoughton, 1909), p. 6.

[23]W. Manson, "Grace in the New Testament," in *The Doctrine of Grace*, ed. W. T. Whitley (London: Hodder & Stoughton, 1922), p. 43.

ruled out. Salvation has its beginning and ending in God's eternal purpose of grace. He loves because he chooses to love; he forgives because it is with him, and of him, to do so. Paul's experience gave him his watchword that God's saving action on man's behalf is "all of grace" and "grace for all" (the theological formulation is to be found in the Epistles to the Romans and Galatians). "The spontaneity and generosity of God's love felt in the act of his salvation, the complete setting aside therein of everything legal and conventional (with, possibly, the added connotation of *charm* of which *charis* is redolent), marked out this word as describing what St. Paul proved of Christ's redemption; under this name he could commend it to the world of sinful men; his ministry 'testifies to the gospel of the grace of God' (Acts 20:24)."[24]

It became clear to Paul, as he mused in the desert of Arabia upon his recent transforming experience, that the freedom of his soul and the forgiveness of his sins were altogether of God's sheer goodness. God's saving action had come to him at a time when he was persecuting the church of God, when he was actually engaged in the evil work of dishonoring the holy name. There was then disclosed to him as an unsought boon God's free pardon; and through the gift of God to his weakness, need, and helplessness he became a new creation of God's infinite grace. Karl Barth asks: What "liberation for new action which does not rest from the very outset and continually on the forgiveness of sins? Who can and will serve God but the child of God who lives by the promise of His unlimited adoption? How can there be a confident expectation and movement in time without the basis of eternal hope? How is there any serious obedience which is not the obedience of faith? As God turns to sinful man, the conversion of the latter to God cannot be lacking. And the conversion of man to God presupposes at every point and in every form that God turns to him in grace."[25]

It also flashed upon Paul in that startling encounter on the highway to Damascus, like lightning in the dark, that his new

---

[24]G. C. Findlay, "Grace," in *Dictionary of the Bible*, ed. James Hastings (Edinburgh: T. & T. Clark, 1909), p. 313.

[25]Karl Barth, *Church Dogmatics* (Edinburgh: T. & T. Clark, 19), vol. 4, pt. 2, p. 505.

instantaneous acceptance by God was his only in the name of Jesus, which he had vowed to discredit. In that shining moment Christ's word from the cross, "Father, forgive"—which Paul may not then have known—and Christ's work on the cross, which climaxed in his exclamation, "It is finished"—the meaning and measure of which Paul was only later to discover—became dynamic in his experience. The truth came home to him, perhaps dimly, but certainly definitely, that God's redeeming mercy was there and then mediated and proffered to him in this Jesus. This experience of grace became Paul's message; the grace which had made him Christian became his essential theology and gospel. For in Christ the grace of God had made the forgiving love of God real to Paul. "What grace implied was the love divine, which is the first thing to be said about the living God."[26] In the benediction of 2 Corinthians (13:14), Paul puts the grace of the Lord Jesus Christ prior to the "love of God and the fellowship of the Holy Spirit." He wishes it understood that it is in the experience of the grace of Christ that there is enjoyment of the love of God in the fellowship created and sustained by the Holy Spirit. The order of the clauses is then to be taken "as a transcript of Paul's own experience: it is through his meeting with Christ, who is all grace, that he entered on a knowledge of the love divine."[27]

For the apostle the love of God is the fount of grace. "Not I, but the grace of God"—this phrase

is very near the heart of the new secret that Paul discovered in becoming a Christian. He had all his life been trying to save himself, to win God's favour by keeping the law and being a good man. But he knew at the bottom of his heart he was not succeeding, though he could not face the fact: and so there was in his life a great deal of what we should call "unresolved conflict." Then in his conversion he learned that he had been making a grand mistake: he had been viewing reconciliation with God from the wrong end. He discovered that God's love for us does not depend on our being worthy of it. We could

[26]Moffatt, Grace, p. 151.
[27]James S. Stewart, A Man in Christ (London: Hodder & Stoughton, 1941), p. 140.

never possibly earn His love by our own goodness, and when we try to make a bad business even of our goodness, becoming at the best self-righteous "Pharisees" such as Jesus disliked (Paul was a Pharisee). But we do not need to earn God's love: He loves us already "while we are yet sinners." It is He that takes the initiative in reconciliation. He has done it in Christ, and it is for us to accept as a free gift what we could never earn or deserve.[28]

Christ's Role in Divine Grace

God's grace is shed abroad and made available in the grace of the Lord Jesus Christ. Thus the apostle sometimes speaks of the "grace of God" (Acts 13:43; 14:26; 15:40; 20:24; Rom. 5:15; 15:15; 1 Cor. 1:4; 3:10, etc.), and sometimes of "the grace of the Lord Jesus Christ" (Acts 15:11; Rom. 16:20; 1 Cor. 16:23; 2 Cor. 8:9; 13:14, etc.). In a few passages, chiefly at the beginning of his Epistles, he associates the grace of God and of the Lord Jesus Christ (Rom. 1:7; 1 Cor. 1:3, etc.). By beginning in this way, Paul declares grace to be the source of all the blessings of the new order which God's unmerited favor brings the redeemed soul. Everything rests on God's free grace in Christ. At the end of his Epistles Paul likewise makes reference to this divine source, as if to make the point that from first to last God's salvation is all of grace.

Moreover, Paul opens his Epistles by connecting "grace" and "peace," usually in the phrase "grace and peace from God the Father and the Lord Jesus Christ." The two terms will also be found at the close, although here they are not always immediately conjoined (see, e.g., 2 Cor. 13:11, 14; Eph. 6:23–24; 1 Thess. 5:23, 28; 2 Thess. 3:16, 18). Thus, as the first word of greeting and the last word of salutation, grace sums up for the apostle the totality of blessings which come from God through Christ. Specifically, grace is the source of the peace of soul enjoyed by the believer. By grace man has peace with God through the Lord Jesus Christ.

In the grace of Christ, Paul discovered salvation and the loving mercy of God. Thus from the very first he found himself compelled to assert the Lordship of Christ (Acts 9:5;

[28]D. M. Baillie, *God Was in Christ* (London: Faber & Faber, 1947), p. 170.

cf. 20, 22). He understood that only Christ can meet man's absolute need of God's absolute forgiveness. Jesus, in whom God has come to us, is the one in whom man meets very God. He who effects such a mediation, and brings to man the reality of God's gracious pardon, must surely be himself of God and for man; he must be, that is to say, at once human and divine. If Jesus were not fully a man, knowing and sharing our human condition and tempted in all points as we are, yet himself without sin, he would be but a shadowy and mythical figure who, while he might somehow have conveyed the illusion of being the Mediator of the new covenant, would be unable to succor those who are tempted. If, on the other hand, he were accorded divine titles merely because his life was Godlike and not because he is actually God, then he would not be for us God present as the conveyor to man of divine forgiveness (see Acts 5:31; 13:38; Eph. 1:7), nor would he be "full of grace and truth" (John 1:14). All that Jesus is and does in his relation to God and man constitutes the definitive self-expression of God towards sinful humanity. In his being and doing he not merely *reveals* God's antecedent forgiving love, but he actually *conveys* to man the reality of the divine forgiveness and renders it possible.

It is in Jesus that we can see God. It is the Christian experience that Jesus is the place where God meets us in grace. The Christian finds in Jesus not simply the basis for a high doctrine of God or for an inspiring faith in God, but the very reality of God himself. In Christ he finds all that he looks for in God. Jesus Christ is all that God can be to us and does all that God can do for us. It is precisely in being himself that Jesus has made divinely available what every man needs of God. His words and actions find their authority and validity in who he is; both converge in bringing men and women into the kingdom of God. It is through him, then, that we are forgiven and inherit eternal life.

We shall later have occasion to say something on what it meant for God to bring to mankind so divine a remission. We must point out here, however, that God's word of forgiveness is for man fully and finally spoken in the deed of the cross. In the declaration of God's forgiveness Calvary has the central part. For Jesus was more than the announcer or reporter of

forgiveness. He was, and he still is, at once its agent and
embodiment. In being uniquely present in Christ's suffering
at the hands of sinful humanity, God revealed the cost which
love could not avoid and bore the judgment holiness could
not overlook to assure to man the divine pardon. Thus God's
grace and the grace of Christ are one in the expression and
exercise of holy love. In the cross there unite God's holiness,
with its aversion to sin, and God's love, with its remission of
the sinner. For what God does involves his whole being. There
is no schism in his nature, no clash of attributes.

Christianity does not with legalistic moralism teach that
forgiveness is hardly possible, nor does it with lawless senti-
mentalism teach that forgiveness is cheaply granted. It teaches
rather that forgiveness is embodied in Christ's atoning cross,
that God's pardon is open to man on the ground of this
supreme revelation of his love, which was made at an infinite
cost and satisfies the inexorable demands of the divine justice
and holiness against human sin. Therefore, as P. T. Forsyth
counsels, we should "remember 1 John 1:9, 'He is faithful and
just to forgive us our sins.' It is in the exercise of His free
faithfulness to Himself and His observance of justice that he
should forgive. It lies in the very holiness that condemns.
There is a similar text in the Psalms, 'Thou art merciful; Thou
givest to every man according to his work.' He is faithful and
just to forgive. There needed no adjustment of His justice
with His forgiveness. So also in Isaiah, 'A just God and a
Saviour.'"[29]

[29]P. T. Forsyth, *The Work of Christ*, The Expositor's Library (London:
Hodder & Stoughton, n.d.), p. 118.

5

Justification and Forgiveness

Justification and Forgiveness—Distinct yet Interchangeable

It is usual for systematic theologians to discuss the forgiveness of sins in the context of the doctrine of justification by faith. But while forgiveness is considered an important aspect of God's justifying act, it is, nevertheless, spoken of as a "negative element" in the process.[1] Indeed, Vincent Taylor makes a sharp distinction between forgiveness and justification, declaring that justification "is more than remission of sins, although it implies and includes this gift of God."[2] On the other hand, E. B. Redlich considers forgiveness to be "full restoration to fellowship" with God.[3] Thomas Watson puts forgiveness in the forefront of justification of the sinner and thus defines justification as "an act of God's free grace, whereby he pardons all our sins, and accepts us as righteous in his sight, for the righteousness of Christ only, imputed to us, and received by faith alone."[4]

[1]Louis Berkhof, *Systematic Theology* (London: Banner of Truth, 1958), p. 514.

[2]Vincent Taylor, *Forgiveness and Reconciliation* (London: Macmillan, 1952), p. 199.

[3]E. B. Redlich, *The Forgiveness of Sins* (Edinburgh: T. & T. Clark, 1937), p. 104.

[4]Thomas Watson, *The Body of Divinity*, 3d ed. (London: Banner of Truth, 1960), p. 157.

In general, then, it seems that forgiveness is conceived negatively, as the blotting out of one's past deeds by wiping the slate clean, while justification is defined positively, as the admission of the forgiven soul into a position of right relationship with God. From the standpoint of theological definition, this distinction may be allowed. But from that of the saving experience, it has little meaning. God's forgiveness is certainly no mere negative affair. He does not, so to speak, pronounce forgiveness from his enthroned remoteness and leave the pardoned sinner outside the door. Quite different, indeed, is the quality of God's forgiveness. For it is the Christian experience that in forgiveness the believer is admitted in Christ into immediate relationship with God himself (Rom. 5:1). Only those who are forgiven in the grace of God's pardon are accepted as righteous and brought into that fellowship by being made partakers of his holiness (Heb. 12:10), for without holiness no one can see the Lord (Heb. 12:14).

As far, then, as God is concerned, for him to forgive is to justify and vice versa. In fact, in Acts 13:38–39, Paul identifies the two—forgiveness and justification. Having stated the basic facts of Christ's death and resurrection, he goes on to affirm: "Let it be known to you therefore, brethren, that through this man forgiveness of sins is proclaimed to you, and by him every one that believes is freed [justified, *dikaioutai*] from everything from which you could not be freed [literally, "were not able to be justified"] by the law of Moses." In his Roman letter the apostle quotes the Old Testament with the same intent. He declares, in the psalmist's words, that the man "whose iniquities are forgiven, and whose sins are covered," is blessed; "the Lord will not reckon his sin" against him, but rather "reckons righteousness [to him] apart from works" (Rom. 4:6–8). Thus H. R. Mackintosh says, "To be justified in the sense that counts for Christian experience is simply to be forgiven and accepted by God."[5] Christ, indeed, "like the more 'evangelical' Old Testament prophets, represents forgiveness as a pure act of grace on the

[5]H. R. Mackintosh, *The Christian Experience of Forgiveness* (London: Nisbet, 1927), p. 3.

part of God, who on the repentance of the sinner receives him graciously and pardons his transgression in the sense of replacing the offender in his former relation of acceptance and favour."[6]

Forgiveness is, then, to be conceived of as the dynamic of justification; it is that act of God which makes justification credible. Forgiveness establishes the relationship which justification declares. "The forgiven man craves to know his permanent status before God. Justification is God's answer to his awakened conscience."[7]

Forgiveness is God's gift of remission to the guilty man. It is not the crediting to him of an innocence that was never his, nor the restoring of an innocence which was once his. God forgives the sinner and thereby opens to him the free actions of his grace. "A forgiven sinner is not regarded by God as one who has never sinned, for that is as impossible as any other contradictory thing. He is regarded as a sinner towards whom God's attitude is no longer determined by his sin."[8] This is the significance of Luther's famous dictum that the believer is "simultaneously justified and a sinner" (simul justus et peccator). By faith in Christ's bearing for us God's righteous judgment on sin the believer is caught up into the righteousness of Christ and is declared acquitted of transgressions and lawbreaking. Thus is the believer declared right before God. He has received a righteousness not of works (Rom. 4:4–5); that is, he has received God's "free gift of righteousness" (Rom. 5:17). Jesus Christ's "act of righteousness leads to acquittal and life for all men" (Rom. 5:18).

The righteousness of God imparted in the righteousness of Christ is the believer's new life-principle. The believer now possesses "the righteousness of faith" (Rom. 4:13; cf. 9:30; 10:6), "the righteousness from God that depends on faith" (Phil. 3:9; cf. Gal. 5:5). In the commitment of faith the forgiven sinner "is not one who is reputed to be, but in his

[6]W. T. Davison, "Justification," in *Dictionary of Christ and the Gospels*, ed. J. Hastings (Edinburgh: T. & T. Clark, 1906), vol. 1, p. 616.

[7]E. Y. Mullins, *The Christian Religion in Its Doctrinal Expression* (Philadelphia: Roger Williams, 1917), p. 54.

[8]W. N. Clarke, *An Outline of Christian Theology* (Edinburgh: T. & T. Clark, 1903), p. 256.

very being as a believer actually is, right with God."[9] For "to believe in Christ and in the sin-bearing love revealed in Him is to do the one right thing for which the situation calls. When the sinner does thus believe he does the one right thing, and it puts him right with God; in St. Paul's language he is justified by faith. God accepts him as righteous, and he *is* righteous; he has received the reconciliation (Rom. 5:11), and he *is* reconciled."[10]

Throughout the preceding pages we have used the terms *pardon* and *forgiveness* interchangeably, and as regards experience this is essentially correct. But a distinction can be made, for each term suggests a particular relation to God. "Pardon is the more frequent official word, but forgiveness is the personal word, expressive of more feeling than often finds its way into the other."[11] More specifically, it seems proper to affirm that "forgiveness" suggests the Father-son relationship between God and man. "Forgiveness is a non-legal term based on the thought of God as Father."[12] Man is an erring and lost son. He was created for sonship, such was his original status before God. Luke 3:38 declares Adam to be "the son of God." This does not mean, however, that man enjoys a natural and continuing filial relationship with God which assures that everyone will be accepted in an automatic divine forgiveness. For it is precisely his sonship which man has defaced, rejected, and sinned away. Nevertheless, the appeal of the gospel focuses on that sonship which once belonged to man. For in responding to Christ as the Son of God man has his sonship restored through the divine forgiveness.

Indeed, virtually all that Christ means and has done for man can be thought of in terms of filial relationship to God the Father. In the apprehension by faith of Christ's atoning death as the Son of God, man is renewed, reconciled (Rom. 5:10), and restored to sonship (Rom. 8:14–16; cf. John 1:12; Rom. 4:6; Eph. 1:8, etc.). It is in this context that the parable

[9] James Denney, *The Christian Doctrine of Reconciliation* (London: Hodder & Stoughton, 1918), p. 291.
[10] Ibid., p. 290.
[11] Clark, *Outline*, p. 256.
[12] Redlich, *Forgiveness*, p. 111.

of the prodigal son has its significance. "Now the ruling idea in the parable of the prodigal son is the idea of the centrality, the completeness, the unreservedness, the freeness, the fulness, wholeheartedness of God's grace—the absolute fulness of it, rather than the method of its action. But however a parable might preach that fulness, it took the Cross and all its train to give it effect, to put it into action, life, history, to charge it with the Spirit."[13]

In both actions of God's grace—forgiveness and justification—the sin of the offender is remitted not because of what he is, but because of what God is. In both actions the past is blotted out. In this regard forgiveness and justification may truly be considered interchangeable. But forgiveness has a more intimate note, while justification brings out more specifically the idea that in the divine pardon the guilt of sin is removed and abolished. Although Jesus used the term *justify* (Matt. 11:19; 12:37; Luke 7:35; 16:15; 18:14), he spoke more often of forgiveness. Paul, on the other hand, in view of his own experience preferred to speak of justification, although he did not discard the term on which his Lord dwelt with such feeling. If, then, forgiveness suggests the filial relationship—God's dealing with the returning sinful child, justification suggests the more legal aspect—God's treatment of the repenting sinner. Justification is tied in with the biblical depiction of God as Judge. Genesis 18:25 affirms that God is the Judge of all the earth, thus, fallen man's "first encounter with God is that of a guilty defendant before a Judge."[14]

Justification is a particular emphasis of the apostle Paul. Indeed, of the thirty-nine occurrences of the verb "to justify" in the New Testament, twenty-eight are in the Pauline letters or in the apostle's recorded words in Acts. The declaration that a man is justified by grace through faith is for Paul the very core of the gospel (Rom. 3:24). "Paul's doctrine of justification is his characteristic way of formulating the central truth that God forgives believing sinners. Theologi-

[13]P. T. Forsyth, *The Work of Christ*, The Expositor's Library (London: Hodder & Stoughton, n.d.), p. 107.

[14]Louis Dupré, *Kierkegaard as Theologian* (London: Sheed and Ward, 1964), p. 84.

cally, it is the most highly developed expression of this truth in the New Testament."[15] The doctrine of justification is for Paul the good news that we can receive from God a full discharge from all our sin and be accepted by him as free from all guilt. This doctrine is Paul's "evangelical message not in part but as a living whole; it is his chosen expression, and no unworthy one, for what God's redeeming love in Christ has done for him. It forms indeed a statement of the Gospel drawn from the nature of the Gospel itself, prolonging the good news announced by Jesus."[16]

In this sense Paul's doctrine comes straight from Christ; and if his word is not precisely that used by Christ, the meaning is the same. For it is of the essence of the Pauline concept of justification that salvation has its source altogether in God and its embodiment in Christ, who has secured for and assured to man the gift of a full pardon. Man has not done, indeed could not do, anything to gain this pardon. Likewise Christ's own statements make clear that justification is not based on personal merit. The lawyer of Luke 10:25 sought to "justify" himself, as did the Pharisees of Luke 16:15. But as the latter passage declares categorically, only God can pronounce a man righteous, for only he knows the true condition of the human heart. The story of the publican and the Pharisee in Luke 18:9–14 is in this regard especially important. The Pharisee tabulated his merits so he could enter a claim that God had an obligation to reward his good conduct. The taxgatherer, knowing himself a sinner, did not, in an effort to offset his evil deeds or to balance the record, make mention of any good deeds he might have performed. Rather, he threw himself on the mercy of God; and as a consequence he, rather than the Pharisee, went down to his house "justified." It is "because he is forgiven that the man goes down to his house 'justified'; and because he has been both forgiven and 'justified' that he is restored to fellowship with God."[17]

The paradox which Paul sets forth, that God justifies the

[15]J. I. Packer, "Justification," in *The Illustrated Biblical Dictionary* (London: Inter-Varsity, 1980), vol. 11, p. 842.

[16]Mackintosh, *Christian Experience*, p. 104.

[17]Taylor, *Forgiveness*, p. 17.

ungodly, is, then, the very paradox which Jesus declared in parable and practice, namely, that the divine goodwill goes out in mercy and forgiveness to those who are unworthy to receive it. Thus Karl Barth can declare, "The forgiveness of sins or justification of the sinner by faith is *the* gift of the Holy Spirit by which all others, so far as they really are that, must submit to be measured; that is the common denominator, so to speak, upon which everything that can seriously be called Christian life must be set."[18]

The Judicial Connotation of Justification

Although the theme of God's justification of the sinner by faith is evident especially in the Pauline writings, it can be found everywhere in the biblical revelation. And everywhere the same judicial connotation is present. Restricting ourselves to the Old Testament term *tsādaq* ("to justify"), we find that the general meaning—"to declare judicially one's state in harmony with the demands of the law" (see, e.g., Exod. 23:7)—has judicial overtones. Some passages put the word in a formal legal (courthouse) setting (Deut. 25:1; cf. Prov. 17:15; Isa. 5:23). There are other texts where the forensic nature of justification comes through. Sometimes God is pictured as having a "controversy" with his people, and the case is conducted in the legal manner of a court (Isa. 1:18; 43:26; Hos. 4:1; Mic. 6:2; cf. Hos. 12:2).

The broad fact that emerges in the Old Testament is that to be justified is to be pronounced not guilty. It is to be cleared of blame. Knowing of God's judgment Bildad the Shuhite asks, "How then can man be righteous [justified, KJV] before God?" (Job 25:4). The question implies that God himself must, and surely will, find a way to clear the guilty. There shines through the Old Testament the hope that he will somehow accept those who cannot claim to have fulfilled the whole round of legal and ceremonial requirements, and so are under divine condemnation. God is a forgiving God, and he will answer the cry of the broken heart (Ps. 51:17). And has not Isaiah a prophetic note of the coming "righteous one" (53:11), God's elect Servant, who will "make many to be

---

[18]Karl Barth, *Credo* (London: Hodder & Stoughton, 1936), p. 153.

accounted righteous," for he shall "bear their iniquities"?
Passages such as Isaiah 43:26 and 45:24 (cf. Ps. 51:4; 143:2)
speak emphatically of God's justification of his people. In
truth, Old Testament prophecy at its profoundest adumbrates
the doctrine of justification through the operation of the
divine righteousness. Despite the sinful condition and utter
unworthiness of Israel, God remained faithful to his promise.
And the fulfilment of his promise is nothing other than the
outgoing of his righteousness in justification of the sinful.

The forensic connotation of the word *justification* is also
evident in Jesus' sayings in the Gospels. He notes wisdom "is
justified" by her works (Matt. 11:19) or by her children (Luke
7:35). The sense of the verb *justify* in both passages is
certainly "to hold or declare righteous," as it is in the
declaration of Matthew 12:37: "By your words you will be
justified." Refuting all those who think they can make themselves right with God, Jesus makes it clear that forgiveness
and acceptance cannot be earned by living up to lofty ethical
and moral standards. Jesus did not present himself primarily
as a teacher of a new and higher morality. He was not, as
some would have it, the founder of a new Judaism, or even the
reformer of the old. This is not, of course, to say that the
ethical precepts he set forth are not profound and solemn,
and that the requirements of the Sermon on the Mount do not
stand as a permanent challenge. Yet when those who believe
that they can secure a passport to heaven by fulfilling ethical
precepts are actually confronted by the various demands for
humility, holiness, meekness, and the like, they will in frustration inevitably ask the question, Who then can be saved?
The whole world stands guilty before God on precisely all
these counts, so that the ethical demands of Jesus, far from
being the gospel of grace, show the overwhelming need of
such a gospel. Christ's activity in behalf of our salvation does
not lie, then, in his insistence upon humility and purity, nor
in his proclamation of the law of kindness and love; it lies
rather in his atoning death on the cross, "in His forgiving
attitude to sinners, and in His wonderful power to convey to
their aching hearts the assurance that His loving mind
towards them [is] the mind of God."[19]

[19]Mackintosh, *Christian Experience*, pp. 105–6.

Note must be taken of how Jesus dealt with his disciples. They were, each one, but simple and sinful men when Jesus first began to associate with them; they were neither pure, nor meek, nor humble. But he did not demand, before he allowed them into his company, that they first adopt his ethical code and strive to fulfil its every requirement. That would have sent them away in despair in the conviction that for them there was no hope of God's salvation. Instead Jesus, "simply by being what he was, . . . gave them the pardoning friendship of God: if we may put it so, He brought them to God by bringing God to them, in a power and reality which awed and cleansed their soul. Salvation met them not as a new requirement, more exacting by far than the old; it was a gift, rather, capable of making them new persons in a new world."[20]

All who, in the days Christ walked the earth, experienced his healing of their soul knew themselves to be put right with God, as did those who received from him the ringing assurance of their sin's forgiveness. The word *justification* they may not have known, but all that the word was later to signify in apostolic proclamation and writing they fully experienced. In its Pauline usage its general meaning is, then, clear enough, while its specifics derive from the apostle's experience of the glorified Lord. In three places the apostle asserts that justification had made him what he was as Christ's man and missionary (2 Cor. 5:16–21; Gal. 2:15–21; Phil. 3:4–14). Paul sets forth justification as an act of divine grace (Rom. 3:24) which nonetheless has a forensic connotation—Christ as our substitute has borne the judgment which God, in accord with his holiness, passes on sin; by the apprehension of faith, believers accept Christ's bearing in their place the judgment of God and are themselves justified thereby. Justification as God's act of acquittal confers on the believer a new standing before God as one fully pardoned. " 'Justification' is not permission to wait in the antechamber, it is admission to the inner presence of God."[21]

[20]Ibid., p. 106.
[21]James Moffatt, *Grace in the New Testament* (London: Hodder & Stoughton, 1931), p. 219.

Justification and Righteousness

To clarify the doctrine of justification, Paul notes how it relates to righteousness, the law, and good works. It was for Paul "a self-evident assumption that righteousness must attach to those who are to obtain salvation."[22] But the questions arise, Whose righteousness? and In what way does it attach itself to the sinner?

In two passages the apostle sets up a contrast between human righteousness—"their own" (Rom. 10:3) and "my own" (Phil. 3:9)—and the divine righteousness—"righteousness based on faith" (Rom. 10:3, 6; cf. 4:11, 13; 9:30) and "righteousness from God that depends on faith" (Phil. 3:9). The burden of the Roman letter, which Paul's own experience had confirmed (Phil. 3), is that a righteousness of one's own cannot save. None among Paul's peers sought more zealously and meticulously than he to be put right with God on the grounds of a righteousness he had himself attained, a righteousness which he thought God must surely reward with a place in his everlasting kingdom. But when overwhelmed in that dramatic hour on the Damascus road by the shining glory of the exalted Jesus, Paul learned that his own boasted goodness was so much dross and got him no marks in the records of heaven.

Yet the rabbinical truth stood that if one is to obtain salvation, there must be a righteousness. Paul discovered in the presence of the living Christ that a righteousness was available to him: the righteousness of God bestowed as a gift (Rom. 5:17). And by that righteousness he was justified. To be justified is, then, in Paul's teaching, to be declared righteous because one has received the righteousness of God in Christ. Our being accepted by God, our righted relation with him, is "all of God's doing" (2 Cor. 5:18). " 'The righteousness of God' is thus a predominantly forensic concept, denoting God's gracious work of bestowing upon guilty sinners a justified justification, acquitting them in the courts of heaven without prejudice to his justice as a Judge."[23]

For Paul the gospel is essentially a disclosure of "the

[22]Mackintosh, *Christian Experience*, p. 114.
[23]Packer, "Justification," p. 842.

righteousness of God" (Rom. 1:17). He uses this phrase when he is concerned with the basis of justification. "Of God" is, of course, a subjective genitive. The righteousness in view is God's own righteousness. It is what God is, his very holiness in loving action. Conferred on the believer, this righteousness of God vindicates his justification of the sinner. It is, then, a righteousness obtained from God, not attained by man.

The righteousness of man and of God stand in the sharpest contrast. To rely on the one is to renounce the other. "If righteousness of man is sufficient, the righteousness of God is superficial; if the righteousness of God is necessary, the righteousness of man can have no place."[24] But only a righteousness as righteous as God himself is acceptable to him. Now man has no such righteousness that can justify him at the bar of God's holiness. He has nothing to present or plead. He must surely be forever doomed unless a way is found out of the impossible impasse. Paul's personal experience afforded him the certainty that there is a way out— God's own gift of a divine righteousness. By exercising faith in God's way of justification one has the assurance that "there is forgiveness, free discharge or pardon, according to the tenor of the Gospel."[25] Being declared righteous by faith, the believer is at once acquitted of his sins and accepted as a forgiven son.

Justification and the Law

Paul also discusses how the doctrine of justification relates to the law. Just as justification does not come by attaining righteousness, it does not come by keeping the law. The subject of the relation between law and gospel is a large one, and it is not our purpose here to investigate its several aspects. But there is one particular point that must be made—the law cannot present a man righteous *coram Deo*. In Paul's own words: "For no human being will be justified in his sight by the works of the law" (Rom. 3:20); "For we hold

[24]James Buchanan, *The Doctrine of Justification* (London: Banner of Truth, 1961), p. 330.

[25]John Owen, *The Forgiveness of Sin* (reprint, Grand Rapids: Baker, 1977), p. 99.

that a man is justified by faith apart from the works of the law" (Rom. 3:28); "Now it is evident that no man is justified before God by the law; for 'He who through faith is righteous shall live'" (Gal. 3:11; cf. 2:21).

If anyone could be justified in the sight of God on the grounds of having fulfilled the law's demands, certainly Paul was such a man. He could truly affirm that he, for his part, was "in legal rectitude, faultless" (Phil. 3:6, NEB). He had reason for confidence if one's standing with God were based on pedigree and performance. For he had lived "righteously," keeping the rules and rituals of his Judaic religion. But deep down in his inmost heart all was not well. There was within an evil self which was at odds with the divine holiness. And the more faithful his observances of the law, the more blatant was the glorification of his own ego, resulting in even greater pride in being a good Pharisee.

In the presence of Jesus, Paul was to learn that that very law which he outwardly boasted he kept so well, when brought into the inner chamber of his soul, showed him up for the sinner that he was. It marked him out as a "lawbreaker" in spite of all his "lawkeeping." What occasion then for boasting? None at all. For the law, instead of offering a real possibility of salvation through fulfilment of its demands in one's own strength, actually inspires a misdirected zeal which results in an arrogant pharisaical attitude of self-justification accentuating one's distance from God.

Not, then, by way of the law can a man be made right with God so as to be accepted of him. To be justified Paul had to die to the law. Instead of justifying him before God in a righteousness obtained by fulfilling its demands, the law turned against Paul and condemned him as a sinner. That justification by reason of which a man is accepted by God does not then derive from the fulfilment of any legal requirements. No man gets to be holy, guiltless, and approved in God's sight as a consequence of things done in obedience to God's law. Only in God's way of a righteousness declared apart from the law can justification come about. In this way there can be a righting of wrong. "Under this divine 'system' a man who has faith is now freely acquitted in the eyes of God by his generous dealing in the Redemptive Act of Jesus Christ"

(Rom. 3:24, *Phillips*). Paul thus became dead to the law by becoming alive to Christ.

Paul learned for himself, and declared to all and for all, that the way of the law is not the way of life. "If a law had been given which could make alive, then righteousness would indeed be by the law" (Gal. 3:21). But righteousness is not by the law, so justification by the law is not an open possibility for any man. In fact, "Christ is the end of the law, that everyone who has faith may be justified" (Rom. 10:4). Man can do nothing towards his justification. It is a matter of sheer grace. Paul consequently heavily accentuates the opposition between the two ways of seeking acceptance with God—the way of law and the way of grace. He shows that the former leads but to condemnation, while the latter issues in life and peace (Rom. 3:20, 28; 5:1; Gal. 2:16, 21; 3:11). He repudiates every attempt to obtain salvation by means of a legal formula on the grounds that every such attempt competes with the absoluteness of Christ. The law condemns, for no man has fulfilled or can fulfil its every demand. The law indeed convicts the erring. But beyond the law provision is made for the overruling of its verdict. Paul declares that justification overturns the judgment of the law (Rom. 8:33–34). The condemned man may find a full pardon, something the law cannot provide. "The free gift following many trespasses brings justification" (Rom. 5:16). Thus in God's gift of grace the sinner under sentence has a full discharge.

Justification and Good Works

Akin to Paul's repudiation of the idea that human righteousness and fulfilment of the law can obtain justification is his rejection of the idea that good works can merit salvation. All three are indeed aspects of the same human endeavor to gain the divine approval in a human way. But Paul denies that works of righteousness or adherence to the law can secure a foothold in the courts of the Most High (Rom. 3:20, 28; Gal. 2:16; 3:2, 5). He is emphatic in declaring that "God reckons righteousness apart from works" (Rom. 4:6), and he appeals to the Old Testament for proof. David, for example, speaks of the "man whom God 'counts' as just, apart from

any specific acts of justice"; such a man rejoices that his
"lawless deeds are forgiven" (Rom. 4:8–9, NEB). And in both
Romans (4:1–5) and Galatians (3:6–9) Paul cites the example
of Abraham to prove that a righteousness based on works will
not justify a man in the sight of God.

In Romans 4 Paul argues that if Abraham had been
justified by what he had done, he would have had some cause
to be proud. Indeed, in what he had achieved he might well
boast, as Paul himself did in his pre-Christian days. But
before God there is no reason for such glorying. For there all
human achievements are as vanity; they are nothing. Paul
proceeds to observe that to consider acceptance with God as
a reward for good deeds would put it in the category of an
achievement—"to one who works, his wages are not reckoned
as a gift but as his due" (Rom. 4:4). This notion that God's
approval can be gained by human endeavor raises several
questions: By what works? How many their number? and
How long must they be performed to earn acceptance with
God? But these are foolish questions, for in no way can man
rise on the ladder of his own righteous deeds to enter God's
sublime abode.

In his letter to the Galatians Paul takes Abraham as proof
of the principle of justification by faith. "Abraham 'believed
God, and it was reckoned to him as righteousness'" (3:6). It
was not, of course, Abraham's faith as such that was counted
to him as righteousness. His righteousness derived from that
on which his faith reposed. Abraham's faith was faith in the
promise of God, a promise which pointed forward to Christ.
Thus Paul can declare that Abraham was justified by faith,
not by works. For Paul all men of faith are sons of Abraham
(3:7), and through their faith they have acceptance with God.
They belong to God because they have faith. Since Abraham
was justified by faith, they that are of faith are Abraham's kin.
In the justification of Abraham God disclosed the one and
only way in which man can be accepted as righteous: by faith.
Thus the gospel as preached beforehand to Abraham and the
gospel as proclaimed by Paul are the same. The man of faith
in the Old Testament and the man of faith in the New are
found to be one in following the same principle as the way to
acceptance with God. "So, then, those who are men of faith

are blessed with Abraham who had faith" (Gal. 3:9). "In Abraham we are blessed, but in what Abraham?" asks Luther; and he answers with Paul, in "the believing Abraham."

That Paul regarded the receiving of the Holy Spirit and the faith leading to justification as one and the same experience is evident in Galatians 3:2. Referring the Galatians to the beginning of grace in their souls, he asks, "Did you receive the Spirit by works of the law, or by hearing with faith?" There is only one answer to such a question. "The law never bringeth the Holy Spirit, but only teacheth what we ought to do; therefore it justifieth not. But the Gospel bringeth the Holy Spirit, because it teacheth what we ought to receive. Therefore the law and the gospel are two contrary doctrines."[26]

On the fact that our justification, our being accounted righteous, is totally a matter of God's doing, Barth makes the following comment (on Question 56 of the Heidelberg Catechism, "What do you believe concerning 'the forgiveness of sins'?"):

> To believe in the Holy Spirit is to hold to what has happened for me in the death of Jesus Christ because of the humiliation of the Son of God. It is to believe that my sins are forgiven, that "for the sake of Christ's reconciling work, God will no more remember my sins . . . so that I may never come into condemnation." The absoluteness of this "never" excludes every anxious look back into the past and every anxious look forward into the future. Anyone who would nevertheless qualify this "never" would in reality set himself in rebellion against the lordship of Jesus Christ, who has decided the fact that *God* accomplishes his own and man's right.[27]

[26]Martin Luther, *The Epistle to the Galatians* (Grand Rapids: Eerdmans, 1930), p. 28.

[27]Karl Barth, *The Heidelberg Catechism*, trans. Shirley C. Guthrie, Jr. (London: Epworth, 1964), p. 87.

6

Guilt and Forgiveness

The Reality of Guilt

The idea and awareness of guilt are universal. Every man at some stage of his life recognizes his responsibility for the performance of acts which in his better moments he judges it was wrong to have done. Paul Tournier is emphatic in this regard. "Guilt," he says, "is no invention of the Bible or the Church. It is present universally in the human soul."[1] Man *qua* man is a moral being with an instinctive recognition of both right and wrong. There is, it seems, in every individual an awareness of the necessity to make a positive moral response in every situation if he or she would be truly human. But everyone is compelled to admit many failures to make such a response. Since we are thus untrue to our own ideal selfhood, there emerges a feeling which on its lower levels becomes a matter of either dissatisfaction with oneself or embarrassment in the presence of others. This consciousness of guilt is due to the fact that human beings "spontaneously feel, after moral failure, that they have gone contrary to what they call their true self, fallen beneath the level of their proper manhood, corrupted somehow the deeper springs of their being. The springs of remorse and the sense of guilt are

[1] Paul Tournier, *Guilt and Grace* (London: Hodder & Stoughton, 1962), p. 123; cf. p. 152.

in part the registering in feelings of the disorder of the whole personality, when the summons of its immanent norm has been disobeyed."[2]

Implied in this remark is the idea that there is an external moral law to which man should conform and an inner requirement that he do so. On both counts man is guilty. He has neither conformed to the law nor willed himself to do so. Thus his guilt is both an objective legal fact and a subjective moral feeling. On the one hand, through the external law, and specifically through our violation of that law, we come to recognize that we are sinners. We are guilty before the law and deserve punishment. In this sense guilt is an objective legal fact; it "is the state of deserving condemnation or of being liable to punishment for the violation of a law or a moral requirement."[3] But guilt is also a subjective moral feeling. "Through the Law alone we can arrive at a knowledge of our guilt, but we cannot have a true perception of our sin. We can be awakened to the burden of our guilt through the Law by itself, but we do not know the enormity of our sins until we are exposed in the light of the cross and resurrection of Jesus."[4] It is only through the law *and* internal consciousness of guilt that we can have a complete view of sin. That we feel guilt within is evidence of our moral responsibility. "Evil has the meaning of evil because it is the work of freedom. Freedom has the meaning of freedom because it is capable of evil; I both recognize and declare myself to be the author of evil."[5] Thus guilt arises from internal consciousness of one's personal responsibility for the wrong done. "It is the man's own fall, and not the fall of his fortunes. It is his moral tragedy, the fall not from happiness but from holiness—the tragedy not simply of gloom but of guilt. Behind all tragedies of incident lies the tragedy of guilt."[6]

[2]H. H. Farmer, *The World and God* (London: Nisbet, 1935), p. 46.

[3]Louis Berkhof, *Systematic Theology* (London: Banner of Truth, 1958), p. 232.

[4]Donald G. Bloesch, *Essentials of Evangelical Theology* (San Francisco: Harper & Row, 1978), vol. 1, p. 97.

[5]Paul Ricoeur, "Guilt, Ethics and Religion," in *Talk of God: Royal Institute of Philosophy Lectures 1967/8*, ed. G. N. A. Vasey (London: Macmillan, 1969), vol. 2, p. 104.

[6]P. T. Forsyth, *The Justification of God* (London: Duckworth, 1916), p. 47.

There is, to be sure, in the Christian understanding of things a certain inevitability about sin. But this does not permit a man to palm off his responsibility. It is true that something beyond and outside man may induce him to wrongdoing. It may indeed even be allowed that "something in sin may be determined by the law of evolution"—something, maybe, "but not the very thing that makes it sin."[7] Evil may show itself present in this form and that: in pride, in social disorder, in evident transgression of the eternal law of right. In whatever form sin may appear, however, each individual member of humanity is aware that he is the cause of his own sin. Although to sin is to do what comes naturally, it is still true that the naturalness of it is no excuse. And although sin is inherent in man's nature, at the same time the individual man finds himself compelled to own responsibility for those actions that express his own sinful selfhood. "This conviction that we are in a state of sin for which we are liable, this direct imputation to ourselves of our sinful being and doing, is the sense of guilt."[8] It is in evil acts that the ultimate truth about our inner selfhood is revealed. For our being is expressed in our doing. "We do not have direct access to this awareness of the guilt of 'being'; we reach it by the more obvious guilt of 'doing.'"[9]

In the last reckoning, it is the individual who is responsible for the deed done. The guilt cannot be referred to the deed itself, as if it were, so to speak, a detachable affair. The person who did the deed must bear the guilt. Moreover, once the deed is performed, it belongs to the past and cannot be undone. Its effects on the individual will be abiding.

Guilt is that element in sin by which it belongs unutterably to the past, and as this unutterable element determines the present destiny of each soul. Guilt means that our past—that which can never be made good—always constitutes one element in our present situation. Therefore we can only conceive

[7]James Denney, *The Christian Doctrine of Reconciliation* (London: Hodder & Stoughton, 1918), p. 197.

[8]H. R. Mackintosh, *The Christian Experience of Forgiveness* (London: Nisbet, 1927), p. 67.

[9]Tournier, *Guilt and Grace*, p. 117.

of our life as a whole when we see it in this dark shadow of guilt. Thus the sense of guilt means that our eyes have been opened to the seriousness of life. The more profoundly serious is our life, the less life is broken up into isolated elements, and the more it is conceived as a whole, the more it is seen in the light of man's responsibility, that is guilt.[10]

Man's past acts are a reality of his present because they are part of the character of that continuing selfhood which is the very essence of what it means to be a human person. The evil actions once done consequently remain in the *now* of one's living. "The guilt of that which has been guiltily done seems to be abidingly contained in the fact of my self-identity with the past."[11]

Yet while guilt is personal in nature and has profound effects on the individual's relationship with himself, it is at the same time "bound up with the activities and relationships of life."[12] No man is an island apart, an isolated unit who neither touches nor is touched by others. There is no such thing as an absolute individual human being whose acts concern himself alone, or only himself and God, should the existence of God be acknowledged. "All are members of a society in which they live, move and have their being morally, and in all they do, of right or wrong, they both affect and are affected by the body to which they belong."[13] This means, as James Denney goes on to observe, that the scope of the sinner's responsibility is enlarged. For a man does not sin to himself any more than he lives to himself. His actions are performed within society and thus have an influence on the society of which he is a member.

The law that determines man's right relationships with his fellows is the declaration, "You shall love your neighbor as yourself." But man fails to fulfil this demand and accordingly is judged guilty in regard to his neighbor. "Man's daily confrontation with the needs and demands of his neighbor is

[10]Emil Brunner, *The Mediator* (London: Lutterworth, 1934), p. 443.

[11]R. C. Moberly, *Atonement and Personality* (London: John Murray, 1913), p. 34.

[12]Gustav Wingren, *Creation and Law* (London: Oliver & Boyd, 1961), p. 176.

[13]Denney, *Christian Doctrine*, p. 191.

a part of this existence of judgment and revelation of guilt."[14] Society by the use of the law—its first use, according to Luther—seeks to compel men to have concern for the needs of others. But the need for compulsion is itself a condemnation. For it indicates that, where possible, we selfishly avoid filling our neighbor's needs. And if we do fill them, we do so stoically in a spirit other than that of love. Guilt arises when a man becomes awake to his own self-centeredness amid the claims of his fellows. Some have designated this a "worldly guilt," an inadequate term inasmuch as it relates merely to the human condition.

The Realization of Guilt

The individual will experience a sense of guilt both in his relationship to himself and in his relationship to society. In the case of the relationship with oneself, a man may know himself in some situation to have failed to live up to what he thought himself to be, a failure of which he feels ashamed. He may indeed openly confess, "I made a mistake," and even allow with Saul, king of Israel, "I have played the fool and have erred exceedingly" (1 Sam. 26:21). But such a confession need carry no moral conviction. One's "guilt" may be a colorless affair, a case of what Paul Tournier calls "false guilt." False guilt relates merely to the act done, but does not reach to the essential self, to the "guilt of being." A person may seek to relieve false guilt by casuistry and rationalization.

Psychologist Carl Jung made much of the idea that the feeling of guilt stems from inability fully to accept oneself. Jung consequently devised his own psychological method for the dispelling of the individual's guilt complexes. But he did not consider that guilt has its basic origin in man's sinful nature. He dealt, then, only with false guilt, not "true guilt," which is the sense of inadequacy which arises upon recognition that the evil of our actions really derives from our sinful nature. Nor did Jung realize that the guilt stemming from inability to accept oneself is also guilt towards God. We

[14]Wingren, *Creation and Law*, p. 180.

recognize, however, that the "guilt towards oneself of the Jung School is indeed at the same time a guilt towards God, since it is the refusal to accept oneself as God wishes us to be."[15]

Similar observations hold in regard to the individual's relationship to society. Here, too, a person's behavior can arouse false guilt, which the Freudians designate "functional guilt" and Martin Buber labels "neurotic guilt." This is the feeling of unease which results from having transgressed some taboo or social code. "Neurotic guilt may be defined as the sense of guilt due to fancied violations of arbitrary norms. It has little to do with the sense of guilt arising from the self's violation of norms accepted by it as valid and validated by the experience of other men."[16] Neurotic guilt can be brought about by the most trivial of issues and in the simplest of ways. Another's silence or look can be taken as disapproval of one's social behavior; this arouses the feeling that one has been guilty of some social transgression. Numerous taboos formulated out of man's social relationships have been set up as prohibitions loaded with menacing dread. Transgressing them can result in so great a feeling of guilt as to cripple an individual's social enjoyment. He will live in constant fear of the anger of others or ostracism. This is, nevertheless, a false guilt because it derives from the mere surface arrangements of social behavior.

There is a more serious guilt feeling experienced in one's relations with his fellows. A man who has acted towards his neighbor selfishly, who has used him as a tool for his own self-gratification and so degraded him, may on reflection feel remorse. He may truly regret his unneighborly conduct and even try to make amends. But this, too, may remain on the level of neurotic guilt, unrelated to the moral law of love for one's neighbor. Tournier points out, "Indeed, any guilt suggested by the judgement of men is false guilt if it does not receive inner support by the judgement of God."[17] The moral law in regard to one's neighbor is related to love of God. Thus

---

[15]Tournier, *Guilt and Grace*, p. 67.

[16]Reinhold Niebuhr, *The Self and the Dramas of History* (London: Faber & Faber, n.d.), p. 23.

[17]Tournier, *Guilt and Grace*, p. 70.

true guilt in relation to wrong done to others is guilt in relation to God. The "guilt towards others of Martin Buber is also guilt towards God since it is a refusal of the divine order in human relationships."[18] "We cannot separate guilt *coram Deo* from a feeling of guilt in regard to our neighbour. . . . Objective guilt *coram Deo* is perceived in man's concrete expressions of guilt, i.e. in his refusal to give what was asked of him, viz. trust in God and love towards his neighbour."[19]

Thus real guilt is more than a personal mistake or a hurt to others; it involves man's relation to God. A false guilt may arise out of a man's relation with himself or society. A true guilt can also arise out of a man's relation with himself or his fellows. But ultimately, true guilt pertains to man's willful repudiation of dependency on God and God's order. This is man's sin and the real source of his guilt. Sin is not only a wrong done against one's self or another; it is ultimately against God.

The essence of objective guilt lies in the breaking of one's relationship with God. "The root of guilt is always to be found in the disruption of fellowship with God."[20] Guilt is man's failure to keep God's law, which is concerned not only with one's relationship with God, but also with oneself and with one's neighbor. Thus that law gives us knowledge of our guilt. This is what Luther called the second use of the law. It is objective guilt "which gives [sin] its power. Its guilt alienates us from God, and it is in virtue of this alienation that sin reigns in us."[21]

The subjective feeling of true guilt arises when we are confronted with the holy demands of God. It is the sense of unease and shame we feel when we are reproached by God in our innermost soul. True guilt leads us to condemn ourselves and to realize that because of sin we are under the righteous condemnation of God as well.

Sin in its essence is mankind's repudiation of his divine purpose: to glorify God and enjoy him forever. This divine purpose, like all of God's purposes, is holy because God is

[18]Ibid., p. 67.
[19]Wingren, *Creation and Law*, p. 180.
[20]Ibid., p. 175.
[21]Denney, *Christian Doctrine*, p. 191.

holy. God's holiness is not a detachable attribute. Rather, his
holiness is his very nature, his essential being. Indeed, "what
is meant by the holiness of God is the holy God."[22] Man's sin
is thus an affront to this divine holiness. It is rebellion against
God as holy being and an infringement of God's glory. Sin
alters man's attitude toward God and consequently affects
both God and man. It is, then, in the context of the personal
relationship between God and man that the real sinfulness of
sin is revealed. "In the light of the Bible 'true' guilt appears as
guilt towards God, a breakdown in the order of man's
dependency towards God."[23] And the more sin is seen as
against God, the truer and sharper is the awareness of guilt.
For "our sense of guilt is due to the presence of the Divine
Holiness."[24] "It is just because the connection between God
and man is so personal that guilt exists, working not merely
causally (as Original Sin, *fomes*), but as the past which affects
the present, and is reckoned as guilt *(reatus)*."[25] Thus, declares
Tournier, "the only true guilt is not to depend on God, and on
God alone."[26]

Sin and guilt are to be understood, then, as pertaining
fundamentally to the breakdown in man's relation to the holy
God. It is of the very essence of holiness to act in revulsion
against all that is not of its own nature. Thus God as holy
being must react to human sin in holy, divine wrath. And
such wrath has powerful effects; it is not just a passion, a
mood, a temper. If we are unaware of the intensity and force
of this wrath, we will not feel true guilt nor seek a better
relationship with God. John Owen declares, "He who is not
acquainted with God's holiness and purity, who knows not
sin's desert and sinfulness, knows nothing of forgiveness."[27]
In Jesus God's holiness has come among men. It is "because
God is so near to us that guilt is so terrible."[28] Thus Peter felt

[22]P. T. Forsyth, *The Work of Christ*, The Expositor's Library (London:
Hodder & Stoughton, n.d.), p. 131.

[23]Tournier, *Guilt and Grace*, p. 66.

[24]Brunner, *Mediator*, p. 444.

[25]Ibid., p. 463.

[26]Tournier, *Guilt and Grace*, p. 69.

[27]John Owen, *The Forgiveness of Sin* (reprint, Grand Rapids: Baker, 1977),
p. 84.

[28]Brunner, *Mediator*, p. 445.

compelled to say in the presence of Jesus, "Depart from me, for I am a sinful man, O Lord" (Luke 5:8).

God's holiness expresses itself in anger against what is not of holiness. God's holy wrath visits judgment upon sin. For if "the essence of God is that he should be holy, it is equally essential that he should judge."[29] To make little of sin is therefore the same as belittling the holiness of God. Man's sin necessarily brings into action that which is essential in God's holiness—his holy judgment on sin. Divine wrath is indeed God's first and fundamental reaction against sin; his holiness entails the deepest revulsion against sin. If any truth about God is obvious it must surely be that his holy wrath against sin involves punishment of it: "in human nature the sense is deeply implanted that guilt demands punishment."[30] God would not be true to himself if he did not take such action against sin. His wrath is thus an objective correlate of human guilt; "only where man recognizes this reality of wrath does he take guilt seriously."[31]

It is only when we consider ourselves in the light of God's holiness that we become seriously aware of our objective guilt. In this light we recognize the inevitability of the divine wrath. "It is the holiness of God that makes sin guilt."[32] God's wrath is the negative aspect of his holiness. Tournier notes that "a God without wrath would be a God without pity. He would be a mere concept of perfection and not a God who saves and suffers, speaks and is moved. He would be a God who passionlessly challenges men, 'You have burdened me with your sins' (Isa. xliii, 24)."[33]

The breakdown in man's relationship with the holy God sets up a barrier between God and man. God's holiness prohibits him from taking sinful man into fellowship with himself. And man's sin precludes him from attaining fellowship with a holy God. Thus "all the world stands hushed and guilty before Almighty God" (Rom. 3:19, LB).

[29]Forsyth, *Work of Christ*, p. 128.
[30]Søren Kierkegaard, *Concluding Unscientific Postscript*, trans. David Swenson and Walter Lowrie (Princeton, N.J.: Princeton University, 1944), p. 459.
[31]Brunner, *Mediator*, p. 445.
[32]Forsyth, *Work of Christ*, p. 79.
[33]Tournier, *Guilt and Grace*, p. 144.

This is true guilt, guilt towards God. All the true guilts which arise out of a man's relationship with himself and with society are ultimately this true guilt towards God. In contrast, then, with false guilt, "'true guilt' is that which results from divine judgement."[34]

The Release of Guilt

It is clear that true guilt arises out of our recognition of our alienation from God due to our failure to keep the moral law, the expression of God's holy will. Any attempt to deal with the problem of guilt which does not get to the root cause will merely increase an individual's despair or inflate his native egoism. For all efforts to improve the human condition by psychological or sociological methods stop short of the deep-rooted guilt of the soul; they are concerned only with the surface guilt. In this area they may have their use and success. For there they function well to destroy unreasonable and unreasoning guilt, helping the individual to accept himself for what he is and adjust to society for what it is.

However, only the healing of the soul which restores a man to a right relation toward God can release him from the burden of his true guilt. But a man cannot be restored to this right relation until he has received God's forgiveness, until for him God "makes death speak of life, defeat of victory, and guilt of pardon."[35] In this restored relationship man discovers he no longer needs to be at war with himself or at odds with society.

The feeling of guilt in the light of God's holiness is then in itself not regrettable. For by it a man may come to admit his unworthiness as a sinner before God and thus to recognize his primary need to be reconciled to God by means of a forgiveness so full that the power of sin is overcome, guilt is annulled, and the pangs of conscience are stilled. True guilt causes the sinner to recognize that he himself is responsible—and answerable—for what he is. His sin is not something to be shrugged off with the cheap remark, "I couldn't help it," or with the easy rationalization, "Well, everyone does it." The

[34]Ibid., p. 67.
[35]H. F. Lovel Cocks, *By Faith Alone* (London: James Clarke, 1943), p. 127.

very awareness of true guilt also leads the sinner to hope for and seek forgiveness. Mackintosh comments: "Our guilty sin can be pardoned: there has taken place a disturbance of our personal relationship with God, and this He can rectify. Indeed, the sense of guilt is of itself a token of hope."[36]

If a man feels no guilt at all for his wrong actions, he has put himself beyond the reach of God's salvation. To sin away all awareness of sin is truly that final sin against the Holy Spirit which has no forgiveness. For that is to lose all sensitivity to goodness and all recognition of sinfulness. That is in truth to call evil good and good evil, and thus to do despite to the Spirit of grace (Heb. 10:29). All sin is indeed forgivable, the sin of all men and sins of all kinds—"all sins—except the sin against the Holy Spirit, against the reality of God himself, when the sinner does not want to be forgiven."[37]

Scripture declares that Esau came to such a state. Falling deeper into immorality and irreligion, he thought to regain his forfeited birthright. But his feeling of guilt was no more than a selfish regret for the things he had lost. His tears were for the treasures he had squandered, and not in the least for the God he had scorned. Esau despised the promises of the covenant and preferred instead worldly plenty; Owen points out that "men who have no desire to be forgiven choose to rest in anything rather than forgiveness."[38] With no feeling of true guilt, Esau did not, and could not, repent with a godly repentance. So he failed to obtain the grace of God (Heb. 12:15–17). Where, however, guilt arises out of a recognition of having disregarded the holy will of God, there is a sign of spiritual and emotional health which can become the spring-board to the discovery of God's gracious pardon. A sense of true guilt drives us to God, who reveals his love in forgiveness. Without such an acknowledgment of guilt there is no opportunity for grace.

The New Testament story of the encounter between Jesus and the woman caught in adultery (John 8:3–11) vividly recounts how the sting and stain of her true guilt were

[36]Mackintosh, *Christian Experience*, p. 66.
[37]Hans Küng, *On Being a Christian* (London: Collins, 1977), p. 274.
[38]Owen, *Forgiveness*, pp. 104–5.

removed and how a sense of true guilt was aroused in her
accusers. The scribes and Pharisees would have had her
condemned out of hand, and they sought to include Jesus in
their number. But instead Jesus gave a totally unexpected
response to the reality of guilt. For Jesus "wipes out the guilt
of the woman who was crushed by it, and arouses guilt in
those who felt none."[39] By the authority of his own person
Jesus pronounced the word of pardon. He did not deny her
guilt; it is obvious that he was aware of it. But he did not
blight her life with condemnation; rather, he blotted out her
guilt with compassion. This is the divine response to acknowledged guilt.

Jesus had already given his response to the woman's
accusers: "Let him who is without sin among you be the first
to throw a stone at her." But none took up the challenge; none
could. One by one they withdrew in shame. The thoughts and
intents of their hearts were brought to light by this word of
Jesus. They had not committed the type of sin which the
woman had, but in other ways their deeds revealed them for
the sinners they were deep down in their being. So Jesus
remitted the guilt of the woman and aroused a sense of guilt
in the others. In this way he demonstrated that no human
individual is free from sin's guilt. Although the moralistic,
self-righteous person tries to conceal the fact, he is just as
guilty as the overt sinner. "In this way," says B. F. Westcott in
a fine comment on the passage, "the words of the Lord
revealed to the men the depths of their own natures, and they
shrank in that Presence from claiming the prerogative of
innocence. At the same time the question as to the woman's
offence was raised at once from a legal to a spiritual level. The
judges were made to feel that freedom from outward guilt is
no claim to sinlessness. And the offender in her turn was led
to see that flagrant guilt does not bar hope. The Law as in a
figure dealt with that which is visible; the Gospel penetrates
to the inmost soul."[40]

For anyone, then, who becomes aware of his guilt and
acknowledges himself to be the sinner he is, there is hope?

[39]Tournier, *Guilt and Grace*, p. 111.

[40]B. F. Westcott, *The Gospel According to St. John* (London: John Murray,
1908), p. 127.

there is promise, there is ground for pardon. By God's grace and love his judgment and wrath can be dispelled. Dealing with our guilt towards God cuts "the Gordian knot of all lesser guilts" because God responds with complete forgiveness for the burdened soul. "Jesus does not awaken guilt in order to condemn, but to save, for grace is given to him who humbles himself, and becomes aware of his guilt."[41] By contrast, the man who tries to relieve himself of his guilt by repressing his conscience or by parading his morality succeeds only in burdening himself the more heavily. Guilt cannot be removed by either the moralism of casuistic law or the round of religious rituals. No monastic display of remorse or show of vaunted impeccability can erase guilt from the soul. To repress one's guilt, to seek to mitigate its sting, to endeavor to pass the blame onto others—these are no solutions. The only way in which guilt can be removed is (and here the psychological and the biblical understanding come together) to accept responsibility in genuine recognition of the guilt as one's own, to repent of the sin that has occasioned the guilt, and to receive the forgiveness of God. "The sinner who has deserved punishment is pardoned: he need only acknowledge the act of grace. Forgiveness is granted to him: he need only accept the gift and repent. This is real amnesty— gratis. He need only live confidently in virtue of this grace. *Grace* then counts *before law.* Or better, what holds is the law of grace."[42]

Only in the free grace of divine forgiveness is the burden lifted and the soul set free. Only as a revelation of God which reason can never fully fathom or the imagination deeply explore, only as a gift, free and gracious, not to be taken for granted, is such forgiveness offered to man. For, says Brunner, "forgiveness can only take place as a real divine act." In this act of forgiveness, as in all his acts, God is involved in all the fullness of his being. This means that his forgiveness "must be of such a kind that will express the reality of guilt, the reality of the divine wrath, and yet, at the same time, the overwhelming reality of forgiving love."[43] It is because God's

[41]Tournier, *Guilt and Grace*, p. 112.
[42]Küng, *On Being a Christian*, p. 274.
[43]Brunner, *Mediator*, p. 449.

grace in Christ meets all these conditions that there is pardon for sinners. "Guilt can only be removed by punishment. Either the sinner himself must bear it, or a substitute must be provided."[44] It is central to the Christian faith, as our last chapter will make clear, that God has provided a substitute. In Christ's own person and work man can find release from objective and subjective guilt. In the words of Augustus Toplady's familiar hymn:

> Rock of Ages, cleft for me,
> Let me hide myself in Thee;
> Let the water and the blood,
> From Thy riven side which flowed,
> Be of sin the double cure,
> Cleanse me from its *guilt* and *power*.

Thus, "the Christian life is one of assured forgiveness of sins, and presupposes the removal both of the sense of guilt and of guilt itself. The believer is taken up into the positive fellowship of eternal life with Christ, in the consciousness of an intimate sonship."[45]

[44]Charles Hodge, *Systematic Theology* (reprint, Grand Rapids: Eerdmans, 1952), vol. 2, p. 532.

[45]C. F. H. Henry, *Christian Personal Ethics* (Grand Rapids: Eerdmans, 1957), p. 381.

7

Experience and Forgiveness

The Importance of Experiencing Forgiveness

"There is not the least encouragement to a sinner," says John Owen, "to deal with God without this discovery of forgiveness in him."[1] For God is known in truth only in the forgiveness of sins. In this knowledge of God as the forgiver of sins all knowledge of him is compounded. "It is, in a word, forgiveness that is with God, and by the exercise of which he will be known to be God."[2] In the experience, then, of God's pardon man comes to know God's basic nature—holy yet loving; judging sin in his righteous wrath, yet forgiving it in his gracious mercy.

It is in the remission of sins that man truly discovers God. Without such an experience of forgiveness a man's ideas of God may be sound enough, but they are merely affirmations of a borrowed creed and a secondhand religion. Such affirmations, true though they be for the mind, will be without that warmth of soul and inward energizing power which make faith real, personal, and creative. For what advantage is it to declare belief in the forgiveness of sins and not to know one's

[1] John Owen, *The Forgiveness of Sin* (reprint, Grand Rapids: Baker, 1977), p. 71.
[2] Ibid., p. 211.

own sins forgiven? Without the experience there is no true
faith, no absolute and dynamic certainty.

"Our certainty of faith is not an impression of Christ," as
merely a great forgiver in his day, "but a life-experience of
Christ."[3] That was the truth Luther learned from his worthy
mentor Johann von Staupitz. Luther knew the creed, believed
it true, and could repeat it accurately; but he did not have the
assurance or joy of knowing his own sins forgiven. To Luther,
Staupitz opened a door of hope and led him to see that it was
not just Peter's and Paul's sins that were forgiven, but his,
too, actually and truly his own. Such a truth about the
forgiveness of sins Luther might have learned from his
reading of Thomas à Kempis, although till his encounter with
Staupitz he would probably have read à Kempis through the
eyes of contemporary Catholicism with its stress on following
Christ's lifestyle—imitating Christ—as a way of obtaining
salvation. But almost on the first page of the *Imitation of
Christ* he would have read, "If thou didst know all the Bible
by heart, and all the sayings of all the philosophers, what
would all that profit thee without the love of God and without
grace?" The sureness of God's forgiveness of the individual is
not to be found in a creed but in commitment. For in the last
reckoning, truths about God and his so great salvation come
from actually experiencing God and his salvation.

Forsyth points out that "our Christian experience tells us
anything it is not about ourselves in the first place, nor about
our creed, but about Christ."[4] The experience of divine
forgiveness points the soul to Christ as the mediator of God's
holy pardon and to God in Christ as saving and redeeming.
Thus the soul can have intimate certainty of creedal formula-
tions. And "where there is an inward, spiritual experience of
the power, reality, and efficacy of any supernatural truth, it
gives great satisfaction, stability, and assurance to the soul. It
removes from the soul the fear of being deceived, and gives it
to have the testimony of God in itself."[5]

[3]P. T. Forsyth, *The Principle of Authority*, 2d ed. (London: Independent,
1952), p. 46.

[4]P. T. Forsyth, *Positive Preaching and the Modern Mind* (London: Hodder &
Stoughton, 1909), p. 67.

[5]Owen, *Forgiveness*, p. 155.

In one of his letters, the poet Keats affirms, "Nothing ever becomes real until it is experienced; even a proverb is no proverb to you till it is experienced." Nowhere is this dictum more relevant than in the matter of divine forgiveness. The gospel message of God's pardoning grace heralded throughout the ancient world brought to men and women an exhilarating sense of being right with God. Those who had opened their lives to his holy pardon were exultant and praised God with singleness of heart (Acts 2:38,47). It is true that as they experienced the certainty of God's forgiveness, these "Christian converts did not find in themselves any immediate abolishing of sins, but they did find an expansion of life as made all things seem possible. As Weinel puts it, 'They *experienced* redemption.'"[6] For Christian faith "properly means an experienced religion of direct, individual, and forgiven faith, in which we are not at the mercy of a priestly order of men, a class of sacramental experts. It is certainty of Christ's salvation at first hand, by personal forgiveness through the cross of Christ in the Holy Spirit."[7] Although we do not intend to admit experience itself as the ground of our authority for God's forgiveness, it is true nevertheless that nothing "can be final authority which is not experienced."[8] Our authority for forgiveness is our experience of faith and belief, which in turn rests on our experience of God himself— the God that he is and has revealed himself to be. Personal forgiveness comes only through the experiences of faith and belief in a God who forgives; "only by believing in a God who forgives sins can we experience the forgiveness of our own."[9] The experience of being forgiven is itself a heartfelt conviction that God does forgive those who come to him in humble trust.

The experience of forgiveness arises, of course, out of the felt need to be forgiven. It is not something imposed regard-

[6]W. M. MacGregor, *Christian Freedom* (London: Hodder & Stoughton, 1931), p. 269.

[7]P. T. Forsyth, *The Person and Place of Jesus Christ* (London: Independent, 1946), p. 12.

[8]Forsyth, *Principle of Authority,* p. 50.

[9]John Baillie, *The Sense of the Presence of God* (London: Oxford University, 1962), p. 64.

less of whether it is desired or not. Nor is pardon "a thing, like money, which can be bestowed or withheld at random. As between God and the spirits He has made, pardon is not a thing at all; it is His taking us back into full, unhampered communion with Himself; it is His inauguration of a relationship between Him and us in which the perplexity and confusion of the bad conscience have vanished, and which in His purpose is characterised by mutual trust."[10]

It seems to be a spiritual law of the gospel that only the man who recognizes that there is something in his makeup which sets him at odds with the holy God will truly appreciate the divine pardon. Only when the inner oracle of a man's heart is awakened to that spiritual sensitiveness which declares him unclean in God's sight is he in a condition to seek forgiveness. In forgiveness God and man are brought together in a true personal relationship and the alienation resulting from man's own act is overcome. "Reconciliation to God comes through God's forgiveness of that by which we have been estranged from God; and of all experiences in the religion of sinful men, it is the most deeply felt and far reaching. We do not need to measure here what is or is not in its power, but every one who knows what it is to be forgiven, knows also that forgiveness is the greatest regenerative force in the life of man."[11] Unless there is forgiveness with God we are all undone. We are without hope in this world, and without preparedness for the next. In view of God's love of holiness, man's only expectation can be of judgment. Yet because of the holiness of God's love he comes to man with the grace of pardon.

For forgiveness to occur, there must be enough of an awareness of the divine severity to drive man to recognize and confess the sinfulness of his sin; man must also have the assurance that God does forgive such guilt. In the union of this recognition of one's sin and this assurance there comes the experience of God's pardon. This implies that there is a requirement for forgiveness and a particular way in which

[10]H. R. Mackintosh, *The Christian Experience of Forgiveness* (London: Nisbet, 1927) p. 238.

[11]James Denney, *The Christian Doctrine of Reconciliation* (London: Hodder & Stoughton, 1918), p. 6.

forgiveness is received, all of which may be summed up in the two great gospel words, *repentance* and *faith*. For, says John Owen, "his [God's] call to repentance is a full demonstration of his readiness to forgive,"[12] and "actual pardon of sin is proposed to faith."[13]

Repentance

The teachings of Jesus as they are recorded in the Synoptic Gospels focus on the kingdom of God. The concept of righteousness holds a central place in these teachings. The righteousness of God requires man to do God's will and so to realize his holy rule in private life and social relationships. But no man has managed to fulfil this requirement—not the best of men, not even those who suppose themselves righteous on the grounds of outward conformity to the moral law. In view of this failure the Bible uniformly declares repentance as a condition of man"s reconciliation with God. The primary significance of the New Testament word "repent" *(metanoeō)*, as has often been pointed out, is "to change the mind." But the sort of change of mind which is in view is in no way as simple as, for example, a request for a second helping of pudding after having just declined it. Rather, repentance connotes a whole new perspective on life and orientation toward a new center. "Are you to learn now what [repentance] is?" asks John Donne. "He that cannot define repentance, he that cannot spell it, may have it; and he that hath written whole books, great volumes on it, may be without it. In one word (one word will not do it, but in two words) it is *aversio* and *conversio;* it is a turning from our sins, and a turning to our God."[14]

Repentance is, then, much more than merely the rejection of one idea for another, the giving of approval to some new or different notion. Repentance as taught by Jesus is a radical revolution in one's view of God and in one's relation to him; it

[12]Owen, *Forgiveness*, p. 137.

[13]Ibid., p. 102.

[14]John Donne, *John Donne's Sermons on the Psalms and Gospels with a Selection of Prayers and Meditations*, ed. Evelyn M. Simpson (Los Angeles: University of California, 1963), p. 217.

is a total change of attitude in regard to him. Just as sin, being rooted in the inner being, goes much deeper than the outward act, so, too, with repentance. It is an inward decision to turn from sin to God; thus it is a life-shaking and soul-shattering revolt. It is an altering of one's view of God which carries with it a heartfelt sorrow for and confession of wrong done. The result is a decisive turning to God and righteousness.

Repentance consequently involves a radical revision of one's "inlook" and outlook. It is a turning to God by turning away from the sin which stands in opposition to all that is of God. As Jesus had much to say about the righteousness of God, he also had much to say about the sin of man. It is in the context of God's righteousness and man's sin that repentance is understood. As the essence of sin lies deep in man's inner life, so must his repentance. It is more than regrets or some deed done. It is other than the mere "sorrow of the world" which "worketh death" (2 Cor. 7:10, KJV). Such sorrow has no relation to God; its only concern is the harmful consequences which one's inconsiderate actions have had upon oneself. But "godly sorrow"—sorrow, that is, being a sinner in God's eyes—works "repentance to salvation" (2 Cor. 7:10, KJV). True repentance is, then, an altering of one's view of God and of sin which involves a turning to God in hope and a turning from sin in horror. It is more than a passing and isolated expression of sorrow.

Repentance is a change of attitude that involves the whole man—his knowing, feeling, and willing. In repentance, "sin is recognized, it is disliked, it is disowned. Recognition by itself is not repentance; it may be defiance. Nor is sorrow for sin repentance, if it be alone of the mind; it may be remorse or despair. Abandonment of sin, by itself, may be no more than prudence. The regenerating fact is all three, as a unity, baptized in a sense of God's personal grace to the sinful."[15]

We are inclined to think of repentance as a once-for-all occurrence, a moment in the religious experience. It has, however, more the aspect of a permanent attitude than a passing agitation. Repentance is a living and dynamic thing, the true nature of which is more evident in its general

[15]Mackintosh, *Christian Experience*, p. 234.

direction than in any transient emotion. Without the desire and intention to abandon *sin* a man's repentance may be no more than an exhibition of that self-disparagement characteristic of human vanity. A man may feel ashamed and truly wish to be free of his *sins*. He may see them as so much surface dirt on an otherwise healthy organism. Yet such acknowledgment of sins may but inflate a man's natural egoism. He will think, "Were I not good at heart, I would not be so distressed; I cannot be entirely graceless, for I have the grace to be ashamed of myself." He may indeed repent of his sins, but that is not the same as to repent of sin!

True repentance or, as the Shorter Catechism has it, "repentance unto life" is something quite different from repenting of specific sins. True repentance "is a saving grace, whereby the sinner, out of a true sense of his sin, and apprehension of the mercy of God in Christ, doth with grief and hatred of his sin turn from it unto God, with full purpose of and endeavour after new obedience." This statement brings to the fore the interiorness of repentance and associates the conviction of sin with the forgiving mercy of God. "Real repentance does not grow quickly. It does not have the automatic character of something psychologically determined. It is only reached after long struggle, after a stormy defence. It is reached, above all, only when conviction of sin grows from within and not from without, when it rises from the depths of our own being, from intimate communion with God, from the prompting of the Holy Spirit, and not from the judgement of men."[16] For the man too proud to acknowledge his sin the Bible holds out no hope. But for the one who owns his unworthiness before God there is the assurance of a free pardon.

Faith

While repentance is the condition on which we receive forgiveness, faith is the way in which forgiveness is realized. The word rings through the New Testament—240 times in

[16]Paul Tournier, *Guilt and Grace* (London: Hodder & Stoughton, 1962), p. 81.

all—as the sole medium by which "all the good that is ours in Christ" (Philem. 6) is secured. So strong indeed is the stress upon faith that James Denney can affirm, "Faith fills the New Testament as completely as Christ does; it is the correlative of Christ wherever Christ touches the life of man." It is not, therefore, "an arbitrary condition on which forgiveness is granted, or on which the reconciliation achieved by Christ is held to apply to sinners; it is that for which Christ, as the author of the work of reconciliation, by the nature of the case appeals, and when his appeal is met by the response of faith, the faith itself is natural, spontaneous, and in a sense inevitable."[17] Thus faith is the whole of Christianity subjectively and Christ is the whole of it objectively.

This juxtaposition of faith and forgiveness is then no artificial arrangement, for the "discovery of forgiveness *is made to faith alone.* The nature of it is such that nothing else can discover it or receive it. No reasonings, no inquiries of the heart of man can reach it."[18] Only in faith is God known; only by faith are contact and communion with him possible. Such faith is not, however, a matter of mere feeling. It is "not a feeling but a verdict. A feeling has causes; a verdict has no causes but grounds."[19] Faith has priority over feeling. In the words of John Owen: "That may be 'believed' which is not 'felt'; yea, it is the will and command of God that faith should stand and do its work where all sense fails."[20]

Faith is not simply the act of an instant; it is rather an attitude which orients the whole of life towards God. It is "the one right thing at the moment when a man abandons himself to Christ, and it is the one thing which keeps him right with God forever."[21] Faith is the one right thing that sets a man right with God. Whereas unbelief means leaving God out of one's reckoning, in faith man reckons on divine grace to bring him into a righted relationship with God whereby estrangement is exchanged for communion. This is what the

[17]Denney, *Christian Doctrine*, pp. 287–88.
[18]Owen, *Forgiveness*, pp. 102–3.
[19]H. F. Lovel Cocks, *By Faith Alone* (London: James Clarke, 1943), p. 72.
[20]Owen, *Forgiveness*, p. 299.
[21]Denney, *Christian Doctrine*, p. 291.

New Testament means by faith. In the sinner's yielding, fully and unreservedly, to the kindness of God there comes release, by means of the cross of Christ, through appropriation of God's free pardon. Faith accepts the gift of God's holy pardon, for "faith finds sweetness and rest in forgiveness with God: it is the only harbour of the soul: it leads man to God, to Christ, as his rest."[22]

In Christ God's forgiveness is offered to man, and by faith it is personally accepted by man. There is no other way, no other means, by which forgiveness can be realized. By faith in the sin-bearing love of God in Christ the believer is reconciled in a full forgiveness. By faith Paul knew himself justified before God in a free pardon. "Before he saw Christ and believed in him he was all wrong with God: God could do nothing but condemn him. Now, in virtue of his faith, he is all right with God, and there is henceforth no condemnation for him."[23] Through faith God's forgiving mercy becomes really and vitally operative in human experience. It is faith which brings healing and pardon to the soul. It is the one key which even in the weakest hand unlocks the treasure house of God's grace. To believe is the one thing a man must do, as it is the only thing he can do to make actual for himself the forgiveness of God.

Where there is no faith, the saving benefits of Christ are of no effect (Rom. 4:14; cf. Gal. 3:17; Matt. 15:6). Not to believe is to be still under the divine condemnation (John 3:18, 36; cf. Col. 3:6; Rom. 8:1; 1 Thess. 5:9). Faith is the medium, the vehicle, the channel whereby the forgiveness of God in Christ becomes ours. Faith is the one thing needful; the one thing a man must do is to believe. And the very least faith makes God's pardon ours because it makes Christ ours. For the realization of that forgiveness the only thing we can contribute is the faith that secures it. This is the one call, the one demand, made upon man. Yet from the natural point of view this is just what man of himself cannot do—except by the Holy Spirit. "If we wish to say what faith is, then we must put all emphasis upon its object. For faith has to do not with

[22]Owen, *Forgiveness*, p. 88.
[23]Denney, *Christian Doctrine*, p. 292.

itself, but with Christ."[24] "It is accordingly," says **B. B.** Warfield, "solely from its *object* that faith derives its value."[25]

A detailed knowledge about Christ is not necessary in order to trust him as the one in whom God meets us in forgiveness of our sin. For while it is by faith that man experiences God's great pardon, it is not the fullness of one's faith but the fact of its presence which secures for him forgiveness. Among those who came to Jesus and were healed by him were some whose faith did not go beyond a belief that he had and was willing to use powers and resources that could meet their need. Their plea for his help amounted to a simple confession that he was different from the common run of religious leaders. They recognized that he taught truths about God with compelling earnestness and also possessed a Godlike compassion for such as sought his aid. Yet their need was deeper than they first realized. And Christ was greater than their intitial faith confessed! To this deeper need some like the paralytic were awakened by Christ's presence and word; they were alerted to that "something" greater about Christ by his assurance that their sins were forgiven. For in forgiveness the believer learns that "all gifts and graces are where Christ is, and faith is the indivisible acceptance of them all in Him."[26] So Christ becomes more and more to believers as in faith they discover that the pardoning mercy of God is a thing more wonderful than they were at first aware. From the earliest stirrings of faith to its final transformation into a clear view of Christ's presence:

> Thou, O Christ, art all I want,
> More than all in Thee I find.

Yet the form of faith does not vary. From beginning to end, from embryo to maturity, faith is trust in Christ and his sin-bearing love.

[24]G. C. Berkouwer, *Justification and Faith* (Grand Rapids: Eerdmans, 1954), p. 175.

[25]B. B. Warfield, *Biblical Doctrines* (New York: Oxford University, 1929), p. 502.

[26]Denney, *Christian Doctrine*, p. 302.

While, as we shall stress in our final chapter, Christ's atoning death is at once the ground on which and the mediation through which God's forgiveness is assured to man, it is by faith in the gracious goodwill of God that the divine person becomes a reality in experience. Although, as R. P. C. Hanson says, "the atonement is not the prelude to our forgiveness but the enactment and focus of it,"[27] nonetheless, the atonement has no effect if there is no faith. Donald Bloesch observes that "we go astray if we assume that we are forgiven no matter what we believe or what we do. God's forgiveness does not become an efficacious reality in our lives apart from faith and repentance. His forgiveness to be sure is more than an offer, but this is only true for those who respond in faith. In faith we discover that we have already been forgiven; at the same time we are moved to appropriate this forgiveness so that it becomes a present saving experience in the here and the now."[28] It is not belief in any special theory of Christ's atoning act that saves, for the one thing needful to that end is faith's apprehension of the loving mercy of God in Christ. It is not belief in the atonement as such that justifies, but belief in the atoning One. Therefore is R. W. Dale, who was himself so concerned to focus attention on Christ's atoning deed, right to insist:

> It is not the theory of the Death of Christ that constitutes the ground of forgiveness, but the Death itself; and the faith, which is the condition on our side of receiving "redemption through His blood," in trust in Christ Himself as Son of God and Saviour of men, not the acceptance of any doctrine which explains how it is that salvation comes to us through Him. For this Trust, it is not necessary that men should acknowledge even the FACT that the Death of Christ is the propitiation for the sins of the world; much less is it necessary that they should receive from others or elaborate for themselves a THEORY of propitiation. It is enough that the authority and love of Christ

[27]R. P. C. Hanson, *The Attractiveness of God* (Richmond: John Knox, 1973), p. 149.

[28]Donald G. Bloesch, *Essentials of Evangelical Theology* (San Francisco: Harper & Row, 1978), vol. 1, p. 164.

have been so revealed to them that they rely on Him for eternal salvation.[29]

In this stress on faith we must guard against the error which would make faith itself a work of merit. True, by faith the gift of God's pardon is secured and made personal, but one's readiness to appropriate a gift is not the reason for its offer. It is no merit to believe, no merit at all to accept a gift. Take the case of a person in need who is offered a sum of money. It is not given to him as a reward for his willingness to accept it. We do not regard the willingness to accept as a work of merit. So is it with faith: there is no inherent meritorious virtue in the act of believing. As eating is the means of bodily nourishment, the "instrument" by which food is assimilated for bodily life, so faith is the means whereby God's forgiveness is realized in experience, the "instrument" by which Christ is received for our spiritual well-being. Faith is not, then, something we bring to God to merit his forgiveness. Indeed, as William Temple affirms, "The only thing of my own which I can contribute to my salvation is the sin from which I need to be redeemed."[30]

It is fatal to the full truth of the Christian doctrine of grace to regard faith itself as a good work which God acknowledges as worthy of reward. Abraham's faith, to which Paul alludes in Romans 4:4–10, was not the reason he was declared righteous. Rather, "faith" is the medium or the instrument by which Christ is received and by which we are united to Him. In Scripture, we are never said to be justified *dia pistin*—on account of faith—but only *dia pisteōs*—through faith—or *ek pisteōs*—by faith."[31] The faith by which God's forgiveness is apprehended is not a natural property of man; it is a trust in God which is granted by sheer grace through the Holy Spirit. "Faith," says Luther (in his "Preface to the Epistle to the Romans"), "is not a human notion or dream, as

[29]R. W. Dale, *The Atonement* (London: The Congregational Union of England and Wales, 1902), p. 314.

[30]William Temple, *Nature, Man and God* (London: Macmillan, 1951), p. 401.

[31]H. D. McDonald, "Justification by Faith," in *Basic Christian Doctrines*, ed. Carl F. H. Henry (1962; reprint, Grand Rapids: Baker, 1971), p. 218.

some take it to be. Faith is a divine work in us, which changes us to be born anew from God." Faith is not generated out of man's own consciousness. It is not the expression of an instinct native to human existence. God "does more than justify faith. He creates it. It is more his than ours. We believe because he makes us believe—with a moral compulsion, an invasion and capture of us."[32]

The saving grace of God's forgiveness, its releasing and transforming virtues, reside not in faith as such, but in Christ. "The saving power of faith resides thus not in itself but in the Almighty Saviour on whom it rests. It is never on account of its formal nature as a psychic act that faith is conceived in Scripture to be saving, as if this frame of mind or attitude of heart were itself a virtue with claims on God for reward, or at least especially pleasing to him (either in its nature or as an act of obedience) and thus disposing him to favour, or as if it brought the soul into an attitude of receptivity or sympathy with God, or opened a channel of communication from him."[33]

At the same time man must himself make the response of faith. God does not believe for man by pushing him off the saddle and riding in his place. God's offered gift to man must be accepted. This, then, is the paradox: man is to believe, to trust, to do what he cannot do, and yet what he can do. The exercise of it, saving faith is an action which cannot be done naturally, and yet which can be done naturally—by the Holy Spirit. This, then, is faith: "admitting Christ to an inward union with your mind and heart and life. By God, who looks on the heart and sees things as they are, the man who has faith is seen as one with Christ, and thus, astonishingly but not immorally, is forgiven."[34]

The Absoluteness of Forgiveness

The divine forgiveness which comes through faith is absolute. God's pardon is not measurable. It is not a case of his forgiveness being less for what men consider lesser sins and

[32]P. T. Forsyth, *The Justification of God* (London: Duckworth, 1916), p. 44.
[33]Warfield, *Biblical Doctrines*, p. 504.
[34]Mackintosh, *Christian Experience*, p. 246.

greater for greater sins. Neither man's sin nor God's forgiveness can be quantitatively calculated. Man, as man, is a sinner whose nature is expressed in acts of transgression of God's holy will. Like a tree planted in desert sand and diseased throughout, so is man in his inner selfhood. However few or many the outward shoots and branches, all men partake of this inner defect. To quote Kant: "From such crooked wood man is made of, nothing straight can be fashioned." For what he is as a sinner and a transgressor, man needs the forgiveness of God, a forgiveness that extends beyond outward acts to include inner being.

Neither does the forgiveness of God come by degrees. It is not, as some have taught, provisional. God does not, so to speak, forgive by installments. He does not provide forgiveness for the sins so far committed and wait to assess its effect before dispensing another dose and then another. The view that God's taking the believer to his heart is a prolonged process of this nature is out of harmony with the declaration, "For I will be merciful toward their iniquities, and I will remember their sins no more" (Heb. 8:12). The forgiveness of God is total and radical, as the parable of the prodigal son (Luke 15:11–32) makes clear. It is a forgiveness once and forever. The transcendent property of this pardoning love is that at the sight of the returning wrongdoer God breaks through the barrier of man's sin and shame and in a free forgiveness restores him fully. The one who knows himself to have sinned much has then this encouragement: regardless of how black the past or how dark the deed there is forgiveness with God.

Looking at the magnitude and manifoldness of his sin a man may indeed hesitate to seek God's forgiveness. He may well feel that his sins are too numerous for God to pardon. Such a man will identify with the amazed wonder and awe which John Donne expressed in his poem "Hymn to God the Father":

> Will Thou forgive that sin where I begun,
>   Which was my sin, though it were done before?
> Wilt Thou forgive that sin through which I run,
>   And do run still: though still I do deplore?

When Thou hast done, Thou has not done,
   For I have more.

Wilt Thou forgive that sin by which I won
   Others to sin, and made my sin their door?
Wilt Thou forgive that sin which I did shun
   A year or two, but wallowed in a score?
When Thou hast done, Thou hast not done,
   For I have more.

I have a sin of fear, that when I have spun
   My last thread, I shall perish on the shore;
But swear by Thyself that at my death Thy Son
   Shall shine as He shines now and heretofore;
And, having done that, Thou hast done;
   I fear no more.

John Donne speaks for every man who has come to know the state of his own true self. There are those sins we can readily acknowledge, for they stand out glaringly. But in the holy light of Christ we find ourselves compelled to say, "I have more." Yet no matter how many more there may be, this word stands sure: "though sin is shown to be wide and deep, thank God his grace is wider and deeper still!" (Rom. 5:20, *Phillips*). For, says God, "I, even I, am he that blotteth out thy transgressions for mine own sake, and will not remember thy sins" (Isa. 43:25, KJV). God declares himself to be a forgiving God who would have men trust him as willing (because of his love) and able (because of his righteousness) to pardon their sin.

The Relationship Between Repentance and Faith

Sometimes repentance and faith, the two necessities on man's side if he is to be forgiven by God, are presented as successive stages or separate acts in the process. Thus some consider repentance a preliminary to the faith by which God's forgiveness is apprehended. Among the great Puritan writers there was a tendency to insist that God's salvation is assured only to those who come to him out of a deep sense of their sinfulness. Thus Thomas Shepherd declares, "It is a

tough work, a wondrously hard matter to be saved."[35] Likewise the Cambridge Platform of 1648 proclaims, "If Christ
has shed seas of blood, set thine heart at rest, there is not one
drop of it for thee, until thou comest to see, to feel, to groan
under this miserable state,—i.e., an overwhelming sense of
sin." These writers, however, consider this sense of sin to be
created by the action of the Holy Spirit.

There are others, of Arminian cast, who also regard repentance as preliminary to faith, but seem to believe that such
repentance is possible for the sinner himself to inspire. On the
other side are those who follow Calvin by putting faith prior
to repentance. Calvin censured "those who think that repentance precedes faith instead of following from, or being
procured by, it, as the fruit by the tree." For no man, he adds,
"can truly devote himself to repentance unless he knows
himself to be of God, except he has previously received
grace." He quotes John 1:13 as proof, with the declaration
that not only does faith always precede repentance, but that
the latter can be procured only by the former. This fact is, for
Calvin, so clearly biblical as to be a matter "without controversy."[36]

Yet perhaps it is better to bring the two into closer connection and consider both as inseparable elements in the total
process of obtaining the justifying forgiveness of God. Although H. H. Farmer contends that faith can be exercised
only in the context of repentance, he could with equal truth
have said that repentance can be exercised only in the context
of faith. He does, in fact, state that the case is not "that we
first repent and then something called forgiveness is added.
The two things, though distinguishable in thought, are given
in a single, inclusive, personal relationship of the profoundest possible kind, the penitence being deeper because the love
of God is already seen to be succouring and forgiving, the
succour and the forgiveness seeming the more wonderful the
more through penitence the soul's complete unworthiness is
felt. It is not possible to be truly penitent in the presence of

[35]Quoted in Sanford Fleming, *Children and Puritanism* (1933; reprint, New
York: Arno, 1969), pp. 19–20.

[36]John Calvin, *Institutes of the Christian Religion*, trans. Henry Beveridge
(London: James Clarke, 1949), vol. 1, pp. 510ff.

the love of God revealed in Christ without experiencing forgiveness and reconciliation."[37] Rather, therefore, "than speak of repentance following faith, as though faith could exist without it, we call it a 'moment' within the unitary act of glad submission to God's lovingkindness, one of a trinity of moments whose other members are reconciliation and hope."[38] Faith orients one toward God, who is at the same time both Judge and Savior. It accepts his judgment on sin and the justice of his wrath, but it also is directed toward his mercy as revealed in Jesus Christ the Lord.

Yet while repentance and faith (it might perhaps be better to speak of repentance-faith) are necessary for the securing of God's forgiveness, they are not themselves its creative cause. The creative cause of forgiveness lies solely in the nature of God: he is at once righteous and merciful, holy and loving.

> God's forgiveness is too often made to appear conditional on man's repentance and decision of faith. Our position is that God's forgiveness, far from being contingent on man's repentance, actually makes genuine repentance possible. Through repentance we discover God's forgiveness and also gain assurance of his favour. Forgiveness is both an attitude and action. God's forgiveness is for all, but the way it is carried out, the way it becomes effective, differs according to the response of the hearer. Yet the response of the hearer by no means creates the divine forgiveness but instead bears witness to it. God's forgiveness does not bear fruit except through man's decision and repentance, but on the other side the latter comes into being by virtue of the prior act of forgiveness.[39]

It is in the experience of forgiveness that all the blessings of the gospel are assured. So can John Owen declare, "It is a great thing to have gospel-forgiveness discovered to the soul in a saving manner."[40] To be forgiven by God, and to know oneself forgiven—that is truly the great discovery of Christian experience. And that is the possibility open to all who in

---

[37]H. H. Farmer, *The World and God* (London: Nisbet, 1935), p. 190.
[38]Cocks, *By Faith Alone*, p. 192.
[39]Bloesch, *Essentials*, vol. 1, p. 214.
[40]Owen, *Forgiveness*, p. 89.

the presence of Christ respond to his forgiving love in repen-
tant faith. "Who that has ever experienced a great forgiveness
does not know that it is the forgiveness itself, and not any
subsequent effort of his own, which is the really creative
thing, the moral power which secures the future?"[41]

In his funeral eulogy for Karl Barth, Hans Küng told of how
he once was discussing with Barth the position of the pope
and the Petrine office of the church. Not able to agree, Küng
said by way of conciliation, "Well, all right, I grant you good
faith." Thereupon Barth became serious and said, "So you
grant me good faith. I have never conceded myself good faith.
And when once the day comes when I have to appear before
my Lord, then I will not come with my deeds, with the
volumes of my *Dogmatics* in the basket on my back: all the
angels there would have to laugh. But then I shall also not
say, 'I have always meant well, I have good faith.' No, then I
will only say one thing, 'Lord, be merciful to me a sinner!'"
Only those who make that plea will know themselves forgiven
and fit to enter the kingdom of heaven.

[41]James S. Stewart, *A Man in Christ* (London: Hodder & Stoughton, 1941),
p. 11.

8

Atonement and Forgiveness

The Necessity of the Atonement

There is forgiveness with God, free and unconditional; this grand gospel truth has been our theme in the foregoing pages. Throughout what has been said this forgiveness has been related to Christ's deed on the cross. In some way, it has been suggested, the death of Christ was necessary for the pardoning act of God. In a verse of Cecil Alexander's well-loved hymn "There Is a Green Hill Far Away," especially favored by children, the connection is stated like this:

> He died that we might be forgiven,
> He died to make us good,
> That we might go at last to heaven
> Saved by his precious blood.

In the simple declaration of the first line, "He died that we might be forgiven," there are brought into association the death of Jesus and the forgiveness of God. The thought is conveyed that God's pardon and Christ's passion are somehow related. There is some vital and essential connection between God's compassion and Christ's cross. In this regard, Emil Brunner declares emphatically, "The Christian doctrine of forgiveness is based upon the fact of atonement."[1] P. T. Forsyth asserts, "Forgiveness through atonement is the essen-

[1]Emil Brunner, *The Mediator* (London: Lutterworth, 1934), p. 516

115

tial of Evangelical Christianity."[2] In a wholly direct sense, "atonement is what it cost God to forgive the sin of the world."[3]

But here questions arise: for example, Why should this be? and How can this be?

There are indeed not a few who would deny that God's forgiveness requires the atonement provided by Christ's death. The important thing about Jesus, they assert, is the message he brought of God's free and unconditional forgiveness. They thus interpret his teaching as going no further than assuring us that God's fatherly goodwill freely forgives all who seek it. For the love of God is such that it reaches deeper than any sin of man and bestows pardon joyously on every penitent sinner. They conclude that to make forgiveness dependent on the supposed sacrificial virtue of Christ's death is a flagrant contradiction of the gospel of God's free love. For, as has been asserted, "Christ never for a moment imagined, any more than the prophets of Israel, that there was any real barrier on God's side to the forgiveness of sins. To Christ and the prophets, repentance and forgiveness were strictly correlative. . . . Neither He nor they thought of anything more than true repentance as necessary for the enjoyment of God's forgiveness."[4] In no way, in this view, does Christ's work provide a basis for forgiveness; it may, at most, simply render man forgivable.

Many of liberal and universalist stance, including the eighteenth-century chemist and clergyman Joseph Priestley, have reasoned that to think that God could not (and would not) dispense his pardoning grace without an atonement is to think meanly of him. They argue that God's command that we forgive others readily must certainly reflect something of the forgiveness of God, in whose image we are created. If a parent can forgive his offending child, and a man his transgressing neighbor, without exacting satisfaction, surely God's forgiveness cannot be otherwise.

[2]P. T. Forsyth, *The Cruciality of the Cross* (London: Independent Press, 1909), p. 1.

[3]H. R. Mackintosh, *The Christian Experience of Forgiveness* (London: Nisbet, 1927), p. 190.

[4]J. Dick Fleming, *Redemption* (London: Hodder & Stoughton, 1921), p. 61.

There are, however, a number of considerations which nullify this contention. It is, of course, agreed that Jesus spoke openly about the forgiveness of God, about a full pardon for men which he pronounced and embodied in his own person. However, during the days he lived on the plane of history, in the restrictions of a peasant existence in Palestine, he could but declare as the gospel for mankind the fact, the general character, and the condition of the divine forgiveness. "The time was not full during Christ's life for preaching an atonement that life could never make."[5] It was not possible at that time to speak openly of the cost of forgiveness on God's side. Not until the event of the cross was itself enacted could the human heart grasp that awful reality. Not in anticipation but only after its achievement could its seriousness and depth be understood.

When Jesus was pressed by his brothers to "show yourself to the world," he could but reply, "My time has not yet come." Not yet could be displayed the grounds of God's free pardon. Not yet could be revealed the heartbreak and the hope, the sorrow and the sympathy, that combine to make the forgiveness of God so wondrous, and so radical, and so lavish. Meanwhile Jesus "could appear to the world as one who went about saying, 'Your sins are forgiven' (John 7:4–5; Mark 2:5). Only on Calvary would people begin to see what that word really meant and cost."[6] The woman caught in adultery had the word of Jesus for her forgiveness, his bare word spoken with authority. But in our case, as Kierkegaard declares, we have a comfort she did not then have. "There is a comfort which did not exist so long as Christ lived, and which he therefore could not offer to anyone: the comfort of his death as the atonement, as the pledge that the sins are forgiven."[7]

The free forgiveness of sins was certainly, as has been said,

[5]P. T. Forsyth, *The Work of Christ*, The Expositor's Library (London: Hodder & Stoughton, n.d.), p. 108.

[6]Ronald Wallace, *The Atoning Death of Christ* (London: Marshall, Morgan & Scott, 1981), p. 45.

[7]Søren Kierkegaard, *Training in Christianity*, trans. Walter Lowrie (London: Oxford University, 1941), p. 270.

the vital spark in Christ's teaching.[8] Nevertheless, the cross was to be the vital spring of that forgiveness. In his death Christ made clear that the divine forgiveness of which he had given assurance did not come about easily. True forgiveness costs; it cost Christ tears and sweat and blood. What then is his atonement, his death on the cross, but the declaration and the display of the cost of forgiveness? For it is "no poor or cheap forgiveness he imparts, but one flowing from unmeasured expenditure of spirit and will."[9]

As there is profound passion in love, so there is profound pain in forgiveness. It is an exacting, a draining thing to forgive a great wrong, to forgive even one great wrong done against oneself. Consider then the wrongs done against God, sins numberless and repetitious. We cannot begin to comprehend the depths of sin's awfulness because we do not have the merest fraction of an idea of sin's meaning and measure. Christ knew it in its full score, in its length, breadth, depth, and height. The Gospel of Mark records that with the cross looming dark before him, Jesus "began to be sore amazed" (14:33, KJV). Luther found these words about our Lord to be most striking. There was nothing in all the world that could amaze the Son of God but the huge totality of human sin. And he had it all "laid upon himself"; "he was made sin" for us. Sin is so exceedingly sinful, so unspeakably evil, that in sore amazement the strong Son of God was crushed down by its pressure and burden unto death and hell.

What do we know about sin? Something of the froth of the cup we know, but of the reality itself we know not the first thing. We know something of its terrible wages; we know something of its sure and full discovery, its dreadful remorse, the day of judgment and the fire that is not quenched, the first and the second death—but all of these are the mere froth on the cup. We still have not come to a knowledge of pure, unadulterated, essential sin, what the apostle calls the sinfulness of sin (Rom. 7:13). Now consider that all of this—the essence of sin and that horrid froth of which we have a little knowledge—was served to Jesus at Gethsemane as he took

[8]See James Denney, *The Christian Doctrine of Reconciliation* (London: Hodder & Stoughton, 1918), p. 16.

[9]Mackintosh, *Christian Experience*, p. 186.

the cup and allowed its poison to bring about his death on the cross. That is the atonement of the cross; that is how God wrought a great salvation for us by the death of Jesus. That is the incalculable cost and the infinite pain of God's holy forgiveness. Thus the "forgiveness of God [rose] up through the depths of a self-abandoning passion such that sinners can never fathom."[10]

There at Calvary all of sin's sting was taken up by Christ, and all of sin's cup of woe was drunk by him to its last dregs. Not a drop has been left for us. At Calvary all of God's holy love was displayed, declared, diffused, as at once amazing and divine. For there Jesus, the very love of God incarnate, bled that he might bless. The cross "means that He, the Forgiving One, really comes to us sinful men. . . . Only when we know Him as the God who thus breaks through can we know Him as the God of Love."[11] What Jesus had done in his lifetime—forgive, and save, and heal—in his death he did with eternal completeness by making visible and valid the glory of God's free grace. Thus did he end his work as he began it. He began it with a call for men to repent and with the promise of divine forgiveness. He ended it with the act of the cross whereby his right and power to bring to man the forgiveness of God were openly established and completely unveiled.

James Denney forcefully exclaims that the necessity of Jesus' death on the cross in order to secure our forgiveness is not inconsistent with the freeness of God's love:

> The love of God, according to Jesus, is no doubt unconditionally free. . . . [At the same time] it is not an abstraction. It does not exist *in vacuo;* so far as the forgiveness of sins is concerned —and it is with the love of God in this relation that we have to do—it exists in and is represented by Jesus' own presence in the world: His presence is a definite character, and with a definite work to do, which can only be done at a definite cost. The freeness of God's love is not contradicted by these facts; on the contrary, it is these facts which enable us to have any adequate idea of what that love really is. To say that it is

[10]Ibid., p. 190.
[11]Brunner, *Mediator*, p. 506.

inconsistent with God's free love to make the forgiveness of sins dependent on the death of Jesus, is exactly the same (in one particular relation) as to say (in general) that it is inconsistent with God's free love that entrance into His kingdom and participation in its blessings should only be possible through the presence of Jesus in the world, His work in it, and the attitude which men assume towards Him. Those who accept the latter should not deny the former. If we give any place at all to the idea of mediation, there is no reason why we should reject the idea of propitiation: for propitiation is merely a mode of mediation, a mode of it no doubt which brings home to us acutely what we owe to the Mediator, and makes us feel that though forgiveness is free to us it does not cost nothing to Him.[12]

This knowledge that Jesus' death was necessary to secure our forgiveness makes us realize all the more our dire need of redemption and forgiveness. For just "as our sense of need for redemption is deepened by our sense of the need for forgiveness, so also in the Christian faith this is deepened still further by our sense of the need for atonement."[13]

To say that God's right and power to forgive were established by Christ's atoning act is at one with saying that whatever it is we as sinners owe to the love of God we owe essentially and finally to the death of Jesus. This is to say that the divine forgiveness is completely different from human forgiveness. It is not merely wider in scope and more generous in expression. Rather, however our human acts of forgiveness may reflect forgiveness, the latter is so qualitatively different from the former that the experience of it is in itself redemptive and restorative. There have been some noble instances of human forgiveness. The wife of an ambassador shot to death in a foreign capital publicly declared her forgiveness of those who perpetrated the crime; likewise the wife of a police sergeant stated that she held no resentment against those who brought about the death of her husband. Their expressions of forgiveness were no doubt honorably spoken and sincerely meant. But the objects of such words of

[12]James Denney, *The Death of Christ* (London: Hodder & Stoughton, 1911), pp. 41–42.
[13]Brunner, *Mediator*, p. 516.

forgiveness were little affected thereby. The evil of their deeds was not wiped out, nor was their lawful punishment mitigated. For a forgiveness which is merely verbal is powerless to remove sin's guilt and cancel its legal sentence. The Bible is emphatic that God overcomes something when he reaches man in forgiveness. His forgiveness is, in Luther's words, a "breaking through wrath," and it is, then, a real and decisive divine action. God's forgiveness is not in word only, but in deed and truth—in the deed of Christ's cross and in the truth of his person. Any "process which begins with denying that we owe to him and to his death the forgiveness of sins, ends up by denying that he has any proper place in the gospel at all."[14]

Forgiveness by Christ is the center of our experience of God's salvation, and the atoning act of Christ is the basis of that forgiveness. The clear biblical truth is that where there is no atonement there is no forgiveness. The cross forever removes doubt about the possibility of forgiveness: "only when Christ is offered as the sacrifice of atonement, not till then, is the comfort at hand which makes the doubt of the forgiveness of sins as impossible—yes, as impossible as it possibly can be; for then it is only for faith that this comfort exists."[15] Thus the deed of the cross is both the simplest and profoundest of all gospel truths. In fact, even the assertion that God is love carries no final conviction apart from this work of Christ. All talk of the forgiving love of God in separation from the cross is vague and unconvincing.

Yet the cross is itself more than a singular display of God's love. It is that, of course: "God shows his love for us in that while we were yet sinners Christ died for us" (Rom. 5:8). But the cross is more than that, vastly more; for here is love in action, here is atonement for sin, here is a death "for us." If indeed the cross be no more than "a kind of practical parable which God set forth of His love and His willingness to save, then when the parable has done its work it can be forgotten."[16] As nothing more than a parable of God's love, the cross would not be nearly enough to meet our case. But it is more;

[14]Denney, *Death of Christ*, p. 43.

[15]Kierkegaard, *Training in Christianity*, p. 271.

[16]Forsyth, *Work of Christ*, p. 102.

it is the foundation on which the new element in Christ's teaching, his assertion of the divine right to forgive, was based. The decisive factor in the gospel is the relation of his death to forgiveness. It thus follows that anyone who proclaims the cross as a demonstration of the love of God, but not as the basis of forgiveness, misses the essential note of the New Testament. "It is not enough to have in the Cross a great demonstration of God's love, a forgiveness of the past which leaves us to fend for ourselves in the future."[17] Nor is it of the nature of the gospel to declare forgiveness of sins as God's free gift of love, without reference to the death of Christ as the way of its procurement and the reason for its offer. It is in the cross that God speaks his pardoning word, and in the redeeming action of his Son he declares our acceptance. For in the last resort, as Brunner affirms, "redemption without atonement is the conception of sin as something natural, like disease," while "forgiveness without atonement means sin is conceived as error."[18] John declares that we perceive the love of God through God's sending his Son to be the propitiation for our sins (1 John 4:10; cf. 2:2). "A God who could do that—a God who could bear the sin of the world in order to restore to man the possibility of righteousness and eternal life—such a God is love. Such love, too, is the ultimate truth about God. But apart from this the apostle would not have said that God is love, nor is it real or specifically Christian for any one else to say so."[19]

It is only a cross-centered gospel that takes seriously man's sin and need. At the cross sin's burden is rolled away. Between Christ's death and his saving work there is, then, a vital connection: it is in this way and at this place that man may come to the kingdom of God as one forgiven. Only in the context of the atoning significance of Christ's death is sense and substance given to the love of God. "The Divine Love is known, by the greatness of the resistance which it overcomes."[20] Only in the cross by means of which God in Christ reconciled the world unto himself can we have any inkling of

[17]Ibid., p. 170.
[18]Brunner, *Mediator*, p. 523.
[19]Denney, *Death of Christ*, pp. 238–39.
[20]Brunner, *Mediator*, p. 468.

the love of God in its measureless length, its boundless breadth, its unfathomable depth, and its infinite height.

> Love proved itself in the passion of Jesus to be the final reality, and no truth which takes possession of the heart of man can ever have power to subdue and reconcile like this. If we wish to experience or to preach reconciliation—which depends on such love—we must not lose the revelation of it by reducing it to a symbol, like the cross, or a dogma, like that of satisfaction: we must keep before ourselves and others the concrete facts in which its reality first came home to men. Christ crucified must be "evidently set forth"—placarded (Gal. iii:1) before men's eyes—that they may receive a due impression of all there is in this wonderful sight.[21]

If, then, there is forgiveness with God at all, it is realized solely on the grounds of Christ's atonement. In his forgiveness of man's sin—in his justifying the ungodly in grace—God must needs act in a manner consistent with his character. He is a God of love, but he is also a God of holiness with whom evil cannot dwell. Therefore, if God in love was to reestablish a relation with man, sin in its every manifestation had to be dealt with in the process by which God mediated pardon to sinners. Only if someone who kept the moral law inviolate bore all of man's sins and thus removed them could God's holiness be satisfied. Hence the necessity of the cross, a necessity which lies deep in the nature of God and in his relation to man. Such is the "must" of Christ's death—"the Son of man *must* suffer many things . . . and be killed" (Mark 8:31; cf. Luke 17:25). The cross is fundamental to God's dealing with sinful man. "Thus this 'necessity' does not proceed from the side of man. We cannot say, 'the Cross "had to" happen!' But the Cross is the only possible way in which the absolute holiness and the absolute mercy of god are revealed together. God cannot make this process 'cheaper.' It really 'costs' so much because of human guilt and Divine Holiness."[22] The cross was thus divinely necessary as the way to the remission of sin. What Christ has done for us had to be done if ever forgiveness was to be ours.

[21]Denney, *Christian Doctrine*, p. 18.
[22]Brunner, *Mediator*, p. 472.

The death of Jesus was indeed, as John tells us in his Gospel, *voluntary*. Christ had in himself the right and the power to lay down his life (10:18). The constraint of the cross was altogether his desire to do the will of his Father out of his love for humankind. Furthermore, his death was *vicarious:* "I lay down my life for the sheep" (10:15; cf. v. 11). That which was necessary to bring lost sheep into the fold he did, doing that which God's holy love required to be done, and which man of himself could never do. There on Golgotha the innocent Redeemer took the place of the guilty. There was love, wondrous love, the love of God, wounded for our transgressions and bruised for our iniquities. In his enduring death for us, the Son of God enabled the divine mercy to liberate us from our guilt, and from the loss and penalty which by the principles of his moral ordering we have incurred by our sin. God's way of forgiveness, the way of Christ's atonement, is the right way, the only way. Finally, John assures us that in addition to being voluntary and vicarious, Christ's death was also *victorious*. For not only had he the power to lay down his life, he also exercised "the power to take it again" (10:18; cf. v. 17).

The thread of salvation through the blood of Christ is woven into all allusions to God's gracious dealings with sinful man. In all these contexts the greatness, the glory, and the grace of the divine Christ shine forth. He, and he alone, has accomplished this stupendous act of redemption for us. There on the cross he is understood. Why the cross? Because the cross is the expression of his greatness: "When you have lifted up the Son of man, then you will know that I am he" (John 8:28). The cross is the key to his glory: "I, when I am lifted up from the earth, will draw all men to myself"(12:32). The cross is the measure of his grace: "As Moses lifted up the serpent in the wilderness, so must the Son of man be lifted up" (3:14). In the cross are the assurance of his greatness, the attraction of his glory, and the atonement of his grace.

Contemplating the cross, Paul says, "Be ye reconciled to God. For he hath made him to be sin for us, who knew no sin; that we might be made the righteousness of God in him" (2 Cor. 5:20–21, KJV). This is too deep, too profound for us. For herein are the mystery, the majesty, and the miracle of

Christ's atonement. Yet this much is plain enough to comprehend and to accept: Christ in his death has brought about a
double identification and a double exchange. In the cross "we
are identified with God's righteousness; Christ is identified
with our sin. There is a double exchange of status: from
sinlessness to that of sin in the case of Christ; from that of
guilt to righteousness in the case of sinners."[23] That is the
wonder of the atonement: the estrangement resulting from
the gulf between God's holiness and man's sin is brought to
an end, and man is restored to fellowship with God in a great
forgiveness.

Biblical Indications of the Relationship Between
Forgiveness and Atonement

It is not our intention to present in this volume a detailed
elaboration of the Christian doctrine of the atonement; that is
reserved for a future volume. However, we must briefly
discuss here what the biblical revelation indicates concerning the relationship between forgiveness and the atonement.

There are a number of passages in the New Testament
where there is a direct link between God's forgiveness and
Christ. It is recorded in the Gospels, as we have noted, that
during the period of his sojourn on earth Jesus pronounced
forgiveness to sin-stricken souls; and in the apostolic preaching forgiveness is specifically associated with his person.
Before the council Peter declares, "God exalted [Jesus] at his
right hand as Leader and Savior, to give repentance to Israel
and forgiveness of sins" (Acts 5:31). At Antioch of Pisidia Paul
declares, "Through this man forgiveness of sins is proclaimed
to you" (Acts 13:38). And he writes to the Ephesians, "God in
Christ forgave you" (Eph. 4:32). Jesus' pardoning of sinners
has its authority in himself. We cannot separate what he
declares from who he is. To receive his word is to receive him.
Therefore to receive his word of forgiveness is to receive him
as the divine forgiver on the basis of who he is and what he
has done for us through the cross.

Jesus came to bring men to the kingdom of God, to grant

[23]John Scott Lidgett, *The Spiritual Principle of the Atonement* (London:
Charles Kelley, 1901), p. 41.

them eternal life through the remission of their sins. But to remit their sins, he had to suffer and die. He had to be "lifted up" on Golgotha's gibbet. His suffering and dying, according to his own word, are vitally connected with forgiveness. "Jesus does not speak of forgiveness as a religious Jew, but as the Messiah who had been sent from God. If his whole message is an 'act of the Messianic consciousness' so much more his language about divine forgiveness."[24]

Jesus proclaimed forgiveness and spoke of God's own merciful action in its bestowal. But the assurance of that forgiveness and merciful action he connected with his own death. When the accounts of Gethsemane and Calvary are read in the light of the words of Jesus himself and of those apostles who received his Spirit, the conclusion is unmistakable: the Messiah had to suffer death so that in his name repentance bringing the forgiveness of sins might be proclaimed to the nations (note how these two ideas are juxtaposed in, e.g., Luke 24:46–47).

There are, in fact, two passages in the New Testament in which the forgiveness of sins is specifically linked to the cross. The first is Matthew's account of the institution of the Last Supper. Words attributed to Jesus himself are recorded. Taking the cup, he bade his disciples drink of it, saying, "This is my blood of the covenant, which is poured out for many for the forgiveness of sins" (26:28, NIV). Only Matthew has this statement which connects the blood of the covenant with the forgiveness of sins. Many New Testament scholars are therefore disposed to believe that the words "for the forgiveness of sins" were not actually spoken by Jesus. The general idea is that they are a later addition made by the church. But while this view may be accepted (although it is doubtful that it must be), it does not cancel out the significance of these words in connecting Christ's shed blood with his pardoning of sin. As Denney explains, "The added words here may be no more than an interpretative expansion of what Christ said, but if they are no more than this they are no less. They are an interpretative expansion by a mind in a position naturally to know and understand what Jesus meant."[25]

[24]Brunner, *Mediator*, p. 538.
[25]Denney, *Death of Christ*, p. 38.

No more cogent is the argument that the "blood of the covenant" had no atoning value. Many scholars believe that the Old Testament background for Jesus' reference to the "blood of the covenant" is Exodus 24, where we read of a covenant made with blood but find no mention of the idea of forgiveness. Their conclusion is that the statement about the remission of sin must be a later addition. There is a more likely background, however, for Christ's reference to a "new" covenant (the qualifying word "new" appears in Luke 22:20). Jeremiah 31 speaks of a new covenant which is specifically connected with the forgiveness of sin (see v. 34). Thus Jesus is definitely proclaiming his death as the condition of sin's forgiveness. "He is establishing, at the cost of His life ['my blood of the covenant'], the new covenant, the new religious relation between God and man, which has forgiveness as its fundamental blessing."[26] The "blood of the covenant" is thus atoning blood with which is associated pardoning power. And it is shed "for many." Here there is a link with Isaiah 53. The one who initiates the new covenant at the cost of his life is the Suffering Servant who in this way justifies many (v. 11). Salvation is based, then, on the death of the cross, and the forgiveness of sinners which is central in that salvation is dependent on the death of Christ.

Like the ransom Jesus paid (Matt. 20:28; cf. Mark 10:45; 1 Tim. 2:6), the shedding of the blood of the covenant is described as being "for many." This phrase does not set a limit to Christ's work. On the contrary, it suggests that the benefits of his self-sacrifice go beyond the lost sheep of the house of Israel. It confirms Christ's own words to the disciples after his resurrection: "It was inevitable that Christ should suffer. . . . So must the change of heart which leads to the forgiveness of sins be proclaimed in his name to all nations, beginning at Jerusalem" (Luke 24:46–47, *Phillips*).

The other passage which links the forgiveness of sins to the cross is Paul's words in Ephesians: "In him we have redemption through his blood, the forgiveness of our trespasses, according to the riches of his grace" (1:7). The phrase "in him" has, according to T. K. Abbott, "a certain argumentative force." It serves to emphasize the exclusion of other

[26]Ibid., p. 40.

possibilities of redemption. It is not apart from him but only in him that this boon of divine grace becomes ours. In him—not in ourselves, nor of ourselves—have we this redemption. The basic idea behind "redemption" is that of deliverance ("release," NEB). Wherever the term appears in the Bible, it suggests setting someone free from a state of servitude by means of the payment of a ransom. The price of our deliverance "in him" is declared in Ephesians 1:7 to be "through his blood"; this phrase states not only the means by which our liberation is secured but also the cost at which it is accomplished (cf. Rom. 3:24–25; 1 Peter 1:18–19). In such a way our rescue was effected, for no one else was good enough to pay the price of sin. This redemption is something "we have"; it is a present reality, for in him "we enjoy our redemption" (*Moffatt*).

The death of the Beloved One secures our redemption, and redemption involves "the forgiveness of our trespasses." Man's sin is so ugly that he can be delivered only by God's act of grace in the deed of the cross. Thus Paul declares that the divine forgiveness is according to the riches of God's grace. Here, then, in this one declaration is enshrined the essence of the gospel of sin's forgiveness. "The premise of the gospel is that we cannot bear that responsibility ourselves; if we are left alone with it, it will crush us to perdition. The message of the gospel, as it is here presented, is that Christ has bourne it *for* us; if we deny that He *can* do so, is it not tantamount to denying the very possibility of a gospel?"[27]

The Atonement as Sacrifice

In the foregoing section we briefly summarized what the biblical revelation has to say about the relationship between atonement and forgiveness. A word must now be added on the nature of Christ's atoning death. Two statements provide the key: Christ died for our sins (1 Cor. 15:3; cf. Rom. 5:6, 8; 6:10, 14–15; 2 Cor. 5:14–15); and he gave himself for us (Eph. 5:2; cf. Gal. 1:4; 2:20). The former of these declarations presents the atoning work of Christ as a *sacrifice;* the latter as a *substitution.*

[27]Ibid., p. 106.

The concept of sacrifice is a fundamental aspect of the New Testament presentation of the death of Christ. While "the necessity for the expiatory sacrifice reveals to us the greatness of the gulf which lies between God and sinful humanity, the reality of the sacrifice also reveals, and not fully till then, what it means to say 'God is Love' "[28] Throughout the Epistle to the Hebrews in particular, the death of Jesus is presented in terms of being a sacrifice. In this context "sacrifice" is the "medium through which a well grounded assurance of pardon is conveyed to the penitent. In Jesus the self-giving of God to man and the self-giving of man to God meet and absorb each other."[29] The Epistle is dominated by the idea that Christ fulfilled all that the Old Testament sacrificial system foreshadowed. In Hebrews he is presented as at the same time the great High Priest (the sole officiant) and the faultless sacrifice (the sole victim) of our great salvation. One telling passage in the Epistle crystallizes the major connotations of the word *sacrifice.* In contrast with the repeated offering of the blood of goats and bulls of the early leviticalism, "How much more, then, will the blood of Christ, who through the eternal Spirit offered himself unblemished to God, cleanse our consciences from acts that lead to death, so that we may serve the living God!" (9:14, NIV). In the exposition of this passage the riches wrought for us by Christ's death are unveiled.

Here is sacrifice at its *fullest:* Christ "offered himself." He came to do the Father's will, and he did it with a veritable passion for obedience. His life was obedience all the way. His obedience began in the "Amen" of the dedication of his life to the Father's purpose, and climaxed in his "Thy will be done," in the full sacrifice of himself to the death of the cross. Both his inner life and outward actions were totally surrendered. The unseen self-oblation of his mind, will, and spirit brought about absolute dedication of his whole being to the Father, dedication climaxed in the death of the cross, wherein Christ experienced the full weight of the divine judgment upon human sin. Thus "surrender was not simply mental; it was expressed in act, in accepted destiny, in the appointment of

[28]Brunner, *Mediator,* p. 486.
[29]Mackintosh, *Christian Experience,* p. 221.

the Father bowed to at whatever cost; it was an inward mind
clothing itself with the vesture of suffering up to and including death."[30] This is what gives the cross its saving efficacy. It
is because of Christ's offering of himself to God that the sinner
can discover pardon.

Here is sacrifice at its *holiest:* "unblemished." The high
priests of the ancient religion were not without their own sin
and shame; but, by contrast, Christ was "holy, blameless,
pure, set apart from sinners" (7:26, NIV). He was "without
spot" (9:14, KJV). There was not a smudge on his holy heart,
not a stain on that shining soul. In him the glory of heaven
strode unsullied through the dirt of earth; he was like a
resplendent diamond in the gutter. His sacrifice "without
spot" was for us with our many spots.

Here is sacrifice at its *costliest:* "the blood of Christ." The
Epistle declares in the light of Calvary that "without the
shedding of blood there is no forgiveness" (9:22, NIV). Here
indeed is the very law of the universe. A grain of wheat must
first fall into the ground and die before it can yield a new
crop. The repeated sacrifices of the old economy had written
deeply on the hearts of God's ancient people the gospel truth
that it is the blood that makes atonement for the soul (Lev.
17:11). The phrase "the blood of Christ" denotes sacrifice of
nobler name and richer blood than they of the former age
knew anything about. For this reason the Epistle unfolds the
greatness and glory of Christ's person (chap. 1; 5:5–10) before
declaring that it was his blood that was shed for the remission of sins.

Here is sacrifice at its *divinest:* "through the eternal Spirit."
Most of the earlier commentators interpret this phrase as
designating either the Holy Spirit or Christ's own divine
nature. Matthew Henry, while apparently preferring the
second alternative, seeks nevertheless to combine both:
"First, it was his *offering himself* to God, the human nature
upon the altar of his divine nature, he being Priest, Altar, and
Sacrifice, his divine nature serving for the first two, and his
human nature for the last. . . . Secondly, it was Christ's
offering up himself *through the eternal Spirit,* not only as the
divine nature supporting the human, but the Holy Spirit,

---

[30]Ibid.

which he had without measure, helping in all, and in this great act of obedience, the offering himself." Recent commentators, however, are less precise. A number of them, following A. B. Davidson's suggestion, link the phrase with the "foreverness" of Christ's high priesthood, and specifically with the declaration of 7:16. The idea, then, is that Christ offered himself to God in the power of his endless life (7:16, KJV). Denney, taking the term "eternal" (*aiōnios*) in the sense of "absolute" or "ideal," says, "What it meant here is that Christ's offering of himself to God had an absolute or ideal character; it is something beyond which nothing could be, or could be conceived to be, as a response to God's mind and requirement in relation to sin. It was the final response, a spiritual response, to the divine necessities of the situation."[31]

But why need we take one of the interpretations and leave the others? Are they not all possible? Are they not all true? For was it not through the Holy Spirit that Christ, of whom the Father said, "Thou art my Son," offered himself to God in the power of his own endless life to be an absolute sacrifice for the sins of the world?

Here is sacrifice at its *fittest:* "cleanse our consciences from acts that lead to death, so that we may serve the living God!" The sacrifices of other days could not do that. The levitical sacrifices purged the flesh; they operated in the region of the outward. Their context was the external. But the blood of Christ, the cleansing and creative grace and power of his atonement, operates on the conscience, to purge it of dead works. "Dead works" are those that defile the spirit and obstruct the free service of the living God. The great truth declared here and elsewhere in the epistle (cf. 10:2) is that once sin is forgiven, the conscience is no longer aware of it. For into the inner recesses of the heart, where no psychological therapies can penetrate, there can come the renewing action of Christ's atoning blood.

We all know something of the shadow on the heart, the self-reproachings of the mind, the pain of conscience that racks our whole being, and the mocking specter of the might-have-been. True, we can and do forget the sinful act which was once so real; the picture fades with time. But

---

[31]Denney, *Death of Christ*, p. 165.

conscience is ever aware of the stain of sin; its haunting and harrowing reality foreshadows the anguish of the great judgment day. Yet the blood of Christ can sweep away this shadowed fear and release the fettered spirit.

Paul, as did our Lord before him, taught us that we are not pure within. Sigmund Freud, Alfred Adler, and Carl Jung discovered this truth, but they did not speak of the "how much more" of Hebrews 9:14. Apparently they did not know that the conscience of the man forgiven through the blood of Christ's sacrifice is purged truly and forever. There is then no need to hark back to the sin pardoned, to the stain washed away; there is no need to lay again the foundation of repentance from dead works (6:1). It is wrong, indeed dangerous to the soul's health, to visit the graveyard of forgiven sin, to tamper with the tomb in which the past is forever buried.

It is the person whose soul has been released, whose conscience has been purged, and whose sin has been forgiven, who can truly serve the living God. Service springs from a spirit of deepening gratitude to him who has given a sense of harmony to our inner world and has made our outer world a sphere where life can be lived to the praise of the glory of his grace. The proof of a pardon which cannot fail, and of a cleansing which no sin can resist, is the testimony of a life spent in glad service to the living God.

Not only the author of the Epistle to the Hebrews, but every writer in the New Testament, conceives of the death of Christ as sacrificial. Paul declares that "Christ loved us and gave himself up for us, a fragrant offering and sacrifice to God" (Eph. 5:2); in 1 Corinthians 5:7 he says, "We Christians have had a Passover Lamb sacrificed for us—none other than Christ himself!" (*Phillips*). The idea of sacrifice underlies John the Baptist's declaration, "Behold, the Lamb of God, who takes away the sin of the world!" (John 1:29), as well as Peter's word that we are redeemed "with the precious blood of Christ, as of a lamb without blemish and without spot" (1 Peter 1:19, KJV). But the conception of Christ's death as a sacrifice for sin is not confined to such explicit statements; it is implied in every other New Testament presentation of Christ's work on the cross. It is indeed not too much to say with Warfield that not only is the doctrine of the sacrificial

death of Christ embodied in Christianity as an essential
element of the system, but in a very real sense it constitutes
Christianity."[32] The centrality of the doctrine of Christ's
sacrifice is evident in various passages which employ the
phrase "the blood of Christ." By "the blood of Christ" come
expiation (Rom. 3:25), justification (Rom. 5:9), redemption
(Eph. 1:7; Col. 1:14; 1 Peter 1:18–19), nearness (Eph. 2:13),
peace (Col. 1:20), purification (Heb. 9:14), cleansing (1 John
1:9), and freedom (Rev. 1:5). All these gifts of God's grace are
realized through Christ's blood of the new covenant shed for
many for the remission of sins. Rightly, therefore, is it said,
"The interpretation of Christ's death as a sacrifice is embed-
ded in every important type of New Testament teaching."[33]
But even more than that, as Warfield is bold to affirm,
"Reiterated reference of the salvation of men to the blood of
Christ is not the only way in which they [the writers of the
New Testament] represent the work of Christ as in its essential character sacrificial. In numerous other forms of allusion
they show that they conceived the idea of sacrifice to supply a
suitable explanation of its nature and effect."[34]

The Atonement as Substitution

The other word essential for a right understanding of
Christ's atonement has been specified above as *substitution*.
Indeed, as A. H. Strong declares regarding the substitutionary view of the atonement, "It furnishes the only proper
explanation of the sacrificial language of the New Testament,
and of the sacrificial rites of the Old Testament, considered as
prophetic of Christ's atoning work."[35] There would seem to be
nothing more evident from a reading of the New Testament
than that its every writer regarded Christ's death as his
taking the place of all humans and bearing for them the
penalty of their sin and guilt. Thus Donald Bloesch can assert

[32]B. B. Warfield, *Biblical Doctrines* (New York: Oxford University, 1929),
p. 435.
[33]W. P. Patterson, *Hasting's Dictionary of the Bible* (Edinburgh: T. & T.
Clark, 1902), vol. 4, p. 343.
[34]Warfield, *Biblical Doctrines*, p. 433.
[35]A. H. Strong, *Systematic Theology* (New York: A. C. Armstrong, 1889),
p. 417.

that "most objective scholars will agree that the theme of vicarious, substitutionary atonement runs through the entire Bible."[36]

It is not required of us to marshal the biblical evidence that Christ died in our stead. That has been well done by others, for example, Albert Barnes in his work *The Atonement*.[37] Commenting on the use of the Greek word *anti* (in Matt. 20:28; cf. 2:22; 5:38; James 4:15), which he insists has always and only the denotation of "in the place of, in the sense of substitution," he affirms, "There is no word in the Greek language that would naturally convey the idea of substitution."[38] To establish that God actually did suffer on the cross in our place, however, we do not need to rely on the usage of the Greek preposition *anti* or *hyper*. For "in the New Testament the cross of Christ is conceived as the self-offering of God. It is God who does it, it is God Himself who suffers, it is God who takes the burden upon Himself. But this act of expiation is real; it *does* something; He suffers; He takes the burden *really* upon Himself; there is a *real* transaction."[39]

"Greater love has no man than this, that a man lay down his life for his friends" (John 15:13); "perhaps for a good man one will dare even to die" (Rom. 5:7). The pages of history are strewn with examples of noble deeds performed in behalf of another. But the greatest benefit accruing to the objects of such regard is at most the prolongation for a while of their human existence. Accordingly, to understand the nobility of Jesus' death, it is useless to examine the records of human behavior, for the death of Jesus is neither illuminated nor illustrated by examples of human nobility. Jesus did not die merely as another volunteer in the regiment of the heroic. His death belongs to another category altogether: "Christ died for the ungodly" (Rom. 5:6); "while we were yet sinners Christ died for us" (Rom. 5:8); "Christ also died for sins once for all" (1 Peter 3:18). Anyone who fails to acknowledge the substitu-

[36]Donald G. Bloesch, *Essentials of Evangelical Theology* (San Francisco: Harper & Row, 1978), vol. 1, p. 148.

[37]Albert Barnes, *The Atonement* (reprint, Minneapolis: Bethany Fellowship, n.d.), pp. 284ff.

[38]Ibid., p. 284.

[39]Brunner, *Mediator*, pp. 482–83.

tionary and penal associations in these and similar statements in the New Testament is guilty of perverse exegesis. As Berkhof declares, "The Bible certainly teaches that the sufferings and death of Christ were vicarious in the strict sense of the word that He took the place of sinners, and that their guilt was imputed, and their punishment transferred to Him."[40]

Jesus did not die to make an impression; he died to effect an atonement. For this reason we must say that the cross is more than the crucifixion. The crucifixion is what men as sinners did to Jesus, the cross is what God as holy love did for sinners. Through the death of the cross God in Christ has made atonement for sin and so obtained for sinful man an eternal redemption. Because of God's divine holiness and justice such an atonement is required, but he has permitted a substitute and in love provided the sacrifice. This, then, is the nature of the atonement: God himself in love has satisfied the ethical demands of his divine nature by substituting Christ's penal sufferings for our just punishment and thus established the grounds for his righteous pardon of human sin and guilt. In a passage in Romans which has often been referred to as the classical New Testament statement on the atonement, a passage which Luther labeled "the very center and kernel of the Epistle and of all Scripture," Paul declares, "For all have sinned, and come short of the glory of God; Being justified freely by his grace through the redemption that is in Christ Jesus: Whom God hath set forth to be a propitiation through faith in his blood, to declare his righteousness for the remission of sins that are past, through the forbearance of God; To declare, I say, at this time his righteousness: that he might be just, and the justifier of him which believeth in Jesus" (Rom. 3:23–26, KJV). These verses expand on the righteousness of God, which is the theme of the whole Epistle. God's righteousness is demonstrated in his setting forth of Christ as a propitiation on behalf of those who have faith in his blood. For by Christ's sacrifice God's righteous judgment is satisfied and sin forgiven. Paul is declaring that God's righteousness is revealed in the means whereby sin is forgiven: the death of

[40]Louis Berkhof, *Systematic Theology* (London: Banner of Truth, 1958), p. 376.

Christ. He "intended, by one single sentence," says Calvin, "to declare that God is propitious to us as soon as we have our trust resting on the blood of Christ."[41]

In a fuller comment Karl Barth declares:

> The propitiation occurs at the place of propitiation—only by blood, whereby we are solemnly reminded that God gives life only through death. Consequently, in Jesus also atonement occurs only through the faithfulness of God, *by His blood:* only, that is to say, in the inferno of His complete solidarity with all the sin and weakness and misery of the flesh; in the secret of an occurrence which seems to us wholly negative; in the extinguishing of all the lights—hero, prophet, wonder-worker— which mark the brilliance of human life, a brilliance which shone also in His life, whilst He lived a man amongst men; and finally, in the absolute scandal of His death upon the Cross. By His blood, then, Jesus is proved to be the Christ, the first and the last word to men of the faithfulness of God. By His death He declares the impossible impossibility of our redemption, and shows Himself as the light from light uncreated, as the Herald of the Kingdon of God. "In the picture of the Redeemer the dominant colour is blood" (Ph. Fr. Hiller), because, in the way of the Cross, in the offering of His life, and in His death, the radical nature of the redemption which He brings and the utter novelty of the world which He proclaims are first brought to light.[42]

In the words of the apostle Peter, "Christ also hath once suffered for sins, the just for the unjust, that he might bring us to God" (1 Peter 3:18, KJV). The just suffered for the unjust. Such is the paradox of the cross in its wondrous exchange: our sin, our shame, our guilt, our punishment have become his; and all that he is—his eternal life, his holiness, his grace, his love—becomes ours "through faith in his blood." His suffering for sin was "once and for all" (RSV). Such is the perfection of the cross; Christ's atonement need not be repeated. It is a finished work. In his death an acceptable substitute was found and a complete sacrifice made. Joachim

[41]John Calvin, *Commentaries on the Epistle of Paul to the Romans* (reprint, Grand Rapids: Eerdmans, 1947), p. 143.

[42]Karl Barth, *The Epistle to the Romans,* trans. Edwyn C. Hoskyns (London: Oxford University, 1933), pp. 105–6.

II Hektor, elector of Brandenburg, demanded of the delegates to the Colloguy of Worms, "See that you bring back that little word 'once'; do not return without it." Christ's atonement is a divine act fully accomplished. There is nothing to be added; there is nothing that needs to be. Nothing now stands in the way of God's forgiveness. There is nothing for man to do to secure God's pardon but to "trust in his redeeming blood" and, in the experience of that redemption, "try his works to do." Christ died to sin once for all (Rom. 6:10), and now he exercises the renewing grace of his endless life. Herein are the ground, assurance, and efficacy of our faith: "the Son of God . . . loved me and gave himself for me" (Gal. 2:20).

There is, of course, far more to be said about Christ's atonement than has been said here. There is certainly more than can be put into a neat and precise formula. But the ideas connoted by the two words *sacrifice* and *substitution* are, we believe, sufficient to clarify the nature of the atonement and to indicate how it satisfies the demands of God's holiness and justice and thus secures our forgiveness. But these are not mere words, mere ideas, mere concepts. They are matters of fact, statements of realities.

As a final statement, we quote the words of an old, much-loved hymn. We glory in their truth. They say all that needs to be known about atonement and forgiveness:

> Bearing shame and scoffing rude,
>   In my place condemned He stood,
> Sealed my pardon with His blood;
>   Hallelujah! what a Savior!